Humphrey
BOGART

Humphrey BOGART

ALAN FRANK

Optimum Books

Photographic acknowledgments
Frank Driggs, New York 10, 11, 12, 14, 16 top, 16 bottom, 17 top, 17 bottom, 18, 23 bottom, 24 bottom, 25, 27 top, 32, 37 bottom, 64; Flashbacks, London 6, 24 top, 34, 37 top, 45, 49, 50, 59, 61, 67; Hamlyn Group Picture Library 27 bottom; Kobal Collection, London 7, 8, 9, 13, 15, 20, 21, 22, 23 top, 26, 28, 29 top, 29 bottom, 30 top, 30 bottom, 31, 33, 35, 36, 38, 39, 41, 42, 43 top, 43 bottom, 44, 46, 47, 48, 52–3, 54, 55, 56, 57, 58, 60, 63, 65, 66, 68, 69, 70, 71, 72, 73, 74, 77; Popperfoto, London 19, 51, 62, 75, 76.

Front cover. Kobal Collection
Back cover. *The African Queen* (United Artists).
Kobal Collection.
Frontispiece. Kobal Collection.

This edition published by Optimum Books 1982

Prepared by
The Hamlyn Publishing Group Limited
London · New York · Sydney · Toronto
Astronaut House, Feltham, Middlesex, England

Copyright © The Hamlyn Publishing Group Limited 1982
ISBN 0 600 37786 5

Printed in Italy

CONTENTS

THE ORIGINAL HUMPHREY BABY

There have been many Hollywood stars who have been accorded legendary status – at least, during their lifetimes. But, in most cases, those legends have been transient ones and simply products of the Dream Factory, as movie moguls and their publicity machines sought to maximize the market value of their most prized – and profitable – properties.

Woody Allen and Diane Keaton before a poster of *Casablanca* in *Play It Again, Sam* (Paramount), the comic adventures of a fan (Woody Allen) obsessed by the Bogart image.

Humphrey Bogart was different. He was already a genuine legend when he died on 14 January 1957. His was a legend that had come from a film career encompassing 80 movies and from his assiduously cultivated off-screen image. And Bogart was unique in that his legend did not die with him. Instead, it has grown to near mythical status and not merely with the kind of star worship tinged with an unhealthy edge of necrophilia that followed the death of James Dean. His continuing popularity derives from the fact that he was probably Hollywood's greatest star, with an abrasive and yet likable persona that touched a chord in filmgoers during his life, and has continued to command respect and reverence in succeeding generations who have known him only through the endless reruns of his movies on television and in retrospective cinema seasons.

In the 1960s, Bogart became an existential hero both in America and Europe, and posters, encapsulating his tough, sardonic yet vulnerable character, have become enduring cult icons. It is a deserved idolization that has spread over into other media, making him one of the most impersonated stars of all time, as look-alikes in television commercials recreate blurred images of Bogart to sell a bizarre variety of products. The enduring quality of his legend was once again confirmed in 1972 when Woody Allen paid homage to the star in the film version of his play, *Play It Again, Sam*, which followed the comic adventures of a movie buff haunted by Bogart.

On screen, Bogart touches a deep chord in all those who see him. This basic appeal was partially summed up by the British film and theatre critic Kenneth Tynan who said: 'We trusted him because he was a wary loner who belonged to nobody, had personal honour . . . and would therefore survive. Compared with many of his Hollywood colleagues he seemed an island of integrity, not perhaps very lovable but at least unbought.'

In some respects, Tynan was wrong. People have been able to see through the deliberate veneer of cynicism and toughness into the basically soft – and even sentimental – person that was the real Bogart. And he certainly belongs to everyone who has ever watched his movies.

Bogart possessed an inner quality that made people both respect and admire him and – as the legions of his impersonators can testify – want to be like him. It is these characteristics that have made him unique and still a major cinema force when so many of his star contemporaries have been forgotten. True stardom is not simply a product of movies – Bogart made his share of stinkers – but is an unrepeatable combination of those movies and, more importantly, of the man who made them.

I saw Bogart briefly as a child in Africa when he was on location making *The African Queen*. Even allowing for hindsight – for I came to see his films much later – he impressed me as a very special man. And, as it has been with others who met him, it is an impression that, through his movies, has become stronger through the years.

Humphrey Bogart was born in New York on 23 January 1899, although later Warner Brothers were to change the date to 25 December 1900, apparently in an attempt to convince the public that, however villainous he might appear on screen, a man who was born on Christmas Day could not be all bad. They also contrived to add an extra inch to his height. These publicity ploys were typical of Hollywood – and typically unnecessary.

His background was one of upper-middle-class wealth. His father, Belmont DeForest Bogart, was a doctor in general practice in a wealthy neighbourhood, having married Maude Humphrey when he was 34. Maude Bogart was, for her time, a remarkably emancipated woman with a lucrative career of her own as a well-known magazine illustrator. They lived in a large house at 245 West 103rd Street in what was then a very fashionable area of New York, and were sufficiently well-off to employ four servants.

They christened their first child Humphrey DeForest Bogart. When he was two, his sister Frances was born and, a year later, Maude Bogart had a second daughter, Catherine Elizabeth.

Bogart made an impression on the public at a very early age when his mother painted his portrait and sent it to a New York advertising agency. His picture was used for the labels and advertisements of the Mellin Baby Food Company and he became famous as the 'Original Maude Humphrey Baby'. There is no record, however, that the infant Bogart ever ate the products he endorsed.

His early childhood appears to have been uneventful. His mother was relatively un-

demonstrative and, in any case, she was wrapped up in her career as an illustrator and subject to frequent and crippling attacks of migraine and the three children saw relatively little of her. In later life, Bogart was quoted as saying: 'I can't say I loved my mother. I guess you could say I admired her.' Dr Bogart, too, was busy with his medical practice, and Bogart would come to react against his father's attempts to direct his life and future career.

The family did go away together for summer holidays in New York State and the young Bogart accompanied his father on hunting, fishing and sailing expeditions. Sailing would become one of his abiding passions in Hollywood and he named his production company *Santana* after his yacht.

Life could not have been all that easy for a boy saddled with his fame as the 'Original

The two-year-old Humphrey, an angelic figure used in advertisements by a baby food company to promote its products.

Maude Humphrey Baby' and the Christian name Humphrey. He was never openly a rebel but he possessed an inherent stubbornness and a toughness which manifested itself in a strong determination to achieve his own self-set objectives. This was a trait that would bring him into conflict with his parents and in particular with his father, who was determined to direct his son's future. The Bogarts intended their son to have a first class education and later to study at Yale. Bogart, however, had other ideas.

When he was almost 14, Bogart was sent to begin his education at New York's Trinity School, a private Episcopalian school on 91st Street. His time there was undistinguished but, outside school, he became a close friend of William A. Brady Jr, the son of the Bogart's next-door neighbour William A. Brady, who had been a boxing promoter and was now a well-known Broadway producer and was married to actress Grace George. Bill Brady Jr was about Bogart's age and, armed with passes supplied by his father, he and Bogart spent weekends together seeing Broadway plays.

In 1917, Bogart was sent to his father's old school, Phillips Academy in Andover, Mas-

Humphrey Bogart and Mary Phillips with Paul Kelly in the play 'Nerves' in 1924. Bogart soon afterwards married Helen Menken, but Mary Phillips became his second wife in 1928.

sachusetts. It was not long, however, before it became obvious that he hated the place. His academic record proved to be a poor one and soon the head of the Academy, Dr Alfred E. Stearns, was forced to warn his parents that unless there were some immediate improvement in their son's work, he would have to leave. No such improvement was forthcoming and finally, in the middle of 1918, Bogart was taken away from Phillips Academy.

In later days Bogart was claimed to have been expelled from the school because of a series of pranks, including ducking one of his teachers in a fountain. Whether or not this were true, it added yet another usable facet to the character of the actor when he was being promoted by studio biographers.

After spending a few weeks in idleness at home, Bogart enlisted in the Navy, lying about his age. Some accounts claim that he sneaked off to join up without his parents' knowledge, but it seems more likely that in fact he had their blessing.

He was a messenger at the training camp and later saw service in the Atlantic on convoy duty on board the troop carrier *Leviathan*, the renamed German passenger liner *Vaterland*.

During active service, Bogart received the wound to his upper lip that left it permanently numb and gave him the lisp that became an essential part of his star persona. Accounts as to how he actually came by the injury vary. One story has it that Bogart was hit by a splinter of wood during the shelling of the *Leviathan* by a German U-boat. Another, more glamorous source, claims that he was struck in the mouth by a handcuffed prisoner he was escorting.

He was honourably discharged from the Navy after the Armistice and returned home, once more coming under family pressure to make something of himself. After a period of idleness at home, he took a number of short-lived jobs, including a year spent working for the Wall Street brokers S. W. Strauss and Company. It was his friendship with Bill Brady Jr that led to his start in show business.

William Brady Sr had embarked on a new career as a movie producer and gave Bogart a job as an office boy with his World Films at Fort Lee, New Jersey. When Brady came into conflict with director Travers Vale over his handling of the 1920 film *Life*, Bogart got his break. Somewhat improbably, Brady told the young man to complete the film, after firing Vale. As a director, Bogart was less than successful and Brady completed the film himself.

Bill Brady Jr's half-sister Alice was a well-known actress and gave Bogart's career

An early romantic lead for Bogart was in 'Hell's Bells', in which he played opposite Shirley Booth on Broadway. Over 25 years later, both were to win Oscars, he in *The African Queen*, she in *Come Back, Little Sheba*.

a new impetus when she suggested to her father that he should be given a job as a stage manager on one of his plays. He received $50 a week as a road manager and, in 1920, went on tour with 'The Ruined Lady' starring Brady's wife Alice George. As well as acting as stage manager, Bogart was required to understudy all the male roles. It was during the tour of 'The Ruined Lady' that he made his acting debut and was quoted as saying: 'I went on the stage for a gag. I'd been kidding Neil Hamilton about the soft life of an actor. "Acting doesn't look very hard to me", I'd said. The funny thing was that that was what I actually thought. The last night of the play, he dared me to go on in his place. I took the dare, and it was all

a horrible fiasco . . . After that experience, I thought "Never again". What changed my mind was finding out that I'd never get rich as a stage manager. I was young and I wanted to get ahead in the world, so I went to Mr Brady and told him my problem. He said: "Why don't you become an actor? Actors earn good money". So, to make a fortune, I became an actor.'

He began to play minor parts, including that of a Japanese houseboy, and eventually was cast as the juvenile lead in 1922's 'Swifty', after an appearance on tour in 'Drifting'. 'Swifty' opened and closed rapidly but at least it earned Bogart his first review from the waspish Alexander Woolcott who wrote: 'The young man who embodies the sprig is what is usually described as inadequte.' Bogart was alleged to have carried this review around with him and, while this critical dismissal increased his mother's desire to see him abandon his new stage career, he persevered.

He went into the play 'Meet the Wife' in 1923, playing a reporter, and the production – with Mary Boland and Clifton Webb – lasted at New York's Klaw Theater for 30 weeks. He continued to learn his trade playing juveniles and minor romantic leads in a series of plays including 'Nerves' (1924), 'Hell's Bells' (1925) and 'Cradle Snatchers' (1925) (Alexander Woolcott decided this time that he was 'adequate', while in Chicago critic Amy Leslie said: 'Humphrey Bogart created a furore . . . He is young and handsome as Valentino, as dexterous and elegant in comedy as E. H. Sothern, and as graceful as any of our best romantic actors'). His other stage work included 'Baby Mine' (1927), 'Saturday's Children' (1928), in which Ruth Gordon made her Broadway debut, with Bogart joining the cast when he replaced actor Roger Pryor, and 'It's a Wise Child' (1929).

During his appearance in 'Nerves' in 1924, Bogart had met actress Mary Phillips and found her highly attractive but, when the play was over, forgot her. And, during the run of 'Drifting', he clashed with actress Helen Menken, culminating in an occasion when, after a series of stage disasters, she struck him.

Clearly it was a case of antagonism making the heart grow fonder. Bogart began to romance Helen Menken, despite the fact that she was older than him and more successful and, after a few weeks, he took out a marriage licence. But, a year later, they were still not married.

Finally, it was Bill Brady who pushed him into matrimony, saying that unless they were married, Bogart would be barred from ever appearing again on the Broadway stage.

The wedding ceremony was a bizarre one. Both Helen Menken's parents were deaf mutes and the ceremony itself – which was held at New York's Gramercy Park Hotel in her parents' suite – was conducted by the Reverend John Kent, who was himself deaf and interpreted the service in sign language. It was an inauspicious start and the marriage

Bogart was compared by one critic to Valentino in the stage production of 'Cradle Snatchers'. Bogart is at the back here, behind Raymond Hackett, Margaret Dale, Mary Boland, Edna May Oliver and Gene Raymond.

One of the first publicity
shots of Bogart the film actor.
He joined the Fox studio in
1930, but found good parts
difficult to come by.

itself was no more successful. The couple fought – verbally and physically – and only lived together for a few months. They were married on 20 May 1926 and, after only a year, Helen Menken divorced Bogart, claiming in the *New York Herald*: 'I tried to make my marriage the paramount interest of my life. Although my career was a success, I was willing to give it up and concentrate my interests on a home. I was deeply interested in acting, but I felt that the managing of a home was something greater. I had planned to make a home for my husband, but he did not want a home. He regarded his career as of far more importance than married life.'

However, Bogart did not remain a bachelor for long. Meeting up with Mary Phillips again, he courted her and the couple were married at her mother's Hartford, Connecticut home in May 1928. This marriage was to last until 1937.

Bogart had made a totally unnoticed screen debut in the ten-minute movie *Broadway's Like That*, filmed in New York in 1930, with Ruth Etting and Joan Blondell.

It was his brother-in-law Stuart Rose who arranged Bogart's first trip to Hollywood.

Rose was working in Fox's New York office and the company was testing a series of Broadway actors for possible screen contracts. He persuaded the head of the New York office, Al Lewis, to see Bogart in 'It's a Wise Child'. Lewis liked what he saw and Bogart was given a screen test.

He had been earning $500 a week on Broadway. His Fox contract paid him $750 a week and, although Mary refused to leave the Broadway play she was appearing in, Bogart took the train to Los Angeles in the belief that movie stardom was beckoning.

It did not take him long to realize that his optimism was ungrounded. Six weeks later he wrote to Rose, complaining of his lot. Bogart had hoped that movies would give him a rest from the kind of young juvenile roles he had been playing on Broadway. His hopes were soon dashed.

His Hollywood career got off to an inauspicious start when he arrived at Fox, expecting to play the lead in *The Man Who*

Came Back. He did not get the part and instead found himself working as vocal coach to the film's star, Charles Farrell.

His first screen role as Tom Standish in 1930's *A Devil with Women* saw him again as a rich young man, this time proving to be a considerable irritation to the character played by star Victor McLaglen, a soldier of fortune engaged in putting an end to the activities of a Central American bandit. The film, properly, belonged to McLaglen, although the *New York Times* said of Bogart that he: '. . . gives an ingratiating performance. Mr Bogart is both good-looking and intelligent . . .'

Although his next picture, *Up the River* (1930) was made after *A Devil with Women*, it was released before it. The film, directed by John Ford, was one that Bogart was later to say that he hated, and it marked the movie debut of another top Broadway actor, Spencer Tracy. Tracy played a convict who, along with his buddy, Warren Hymer, helps fellow convict Bogart, serving a sentence for accidental manslaughter, to clear up his problems and get the girl – played by Claire Luce – before the two return to jail in order to ensure that the prisoners win an important baseball game. The movie emerged as broad comedy and did nothing to further Bogart's screen career.

Fox then put him into director Alfred Santell's *Body and Soul* (1931), where he played a young American flyer with the Royal Air Force in France. The film starred Bogart's one-time voice pupil Charles Farrell, and the

Bogart's first 'part' in Hollywood was as vocal coach to Charles Farrell. When later they appeared together in *Body and Soul* (Fox), there was friction, but in time they became friends.

two were openly hostile during filming, although subsequently they became friends.

His next part was a small one in the remake of Universal's 1924 success *The Flirt*, now retitled *Bad Sister*. Bogart was loaned to Universal by Fox for the picture, which marked Bette Davis' screen debut and again it did nothing to enhance his prospects.

It soon became clear that Fox had little interest in the new contract player. He rejoined Victor McLaglen in a bit part in *Women of All Nations*, playing a buddy of McLaglen and Edmund Lowe, who were recreating the characters of Sergeant Flagg and Sergeant Quirt which they had popularized in *What Price Glory?* in 1926. They had the screen practically to themselves, Bogart being relegated to number nine in the cast

list, below, among others, Bela Lugosi. He was only seen briefly and, indeed, vanished altogether from some release prints.

Bad Sister, *Women of All Nations* and Bogart's final film for Fox were all released in 1931. This last movie was a Western, *A Holy Terror*, directed by Irving Cummings, who had helmed Bogart's first Hollywood movie, *A Devil with Women*. George Brent was the star and Bogart played ranch foreman Steve Nash. Bogart did not enjoy making the movie, later claiming that, because he was too short, the studio had fitted him with elevator shoes and padded his shoulders to make him look taller. Quoted as saying: 'I spent a very unsuccessful year at Fox', Bogart returned to Broadway, now quite convinced that the stage was his real metier.

Bette Davis made her film debut a year after Bogart in *Bad Sister* (Universal). Bogart was also in the film. With them in this scene are Sidney Fox and Conrad Nagel.

HOLLYWOOD TO BROADWAY AND BACK

Bogart returned to the New York stage in 1931 and appeared in 'After All' with Helen Haye and Margaret Perry. His lack of success continued, as the play ran for fewer than 100 performances.

His return to New York soon turned sour. Before going to Hollywood, he and Mary had agreed that they were adults and sophisticated and that, should the opportunity arise for a little extramarital dalliance, no harm would be done. Bogart had not been a saint in Hollywood but he was shocked and hurt when Mary confessed that she had fallen in love with actor Roland Young. Nevertheless, they were able to patch up their marriage and Bogart started to look for a play.

Right: Back to films in 1932, Bogart starred as an inventor in *Love Affair* (Columbia), but was merely a romantic foil for Dorothy MacKaill.

However, the Depression was at its height and the generally straightened circumstances it brought about had affected the Broadway scene. When he succeeded in getting a part in John Van Druten's play 'After All' in 1931, it was not a success. Luckily, he was offered a six-month contract back in Hollywood with Columbia, left 'After All' and headed back West once more.

Harry Cohn, Columbia's much hated head – with whom Bogart got on, however – put him into *Love Affair* (1932), giving him his first starring role, although, in the film that emerged, he was merely seen as a support for English actress Dorothy MacKaill who was trying to break into talking pictures after a career as a silent star and a Ziegfeld dancer. He played an inventor-cum-flying instructor who becomes romantically entangled with pupil MacKaill and again the picture did nothing for him – or, indeed, for the studio, Columbia.

After *Love Affair*, he went to Warners – the studio that later would be associated with most of his greatest successes – to make 1932's *Big City Blues* and *Three on a Match*. In the first, directed by Mervyn LeRoy, Bogart received tenth billing, the stars being Joan Blondell – with whom he had made his movie debut – and Eric Linden. *Big City Blues* followed the adventures of country boy Linden in the big, bad world of New York – and followed the rest of Bogart's film career into oblivion. *Three on a Match* at least gave him his first gangster role, which he played with verve, but the part was small, the movie concentrating, once more under LeRoy's direction, on the fortunes of a trio of young women – Joan Blondell, Ann Dvorak and Bette Davis – a decade after leaving college.

Once again, Bogart went back to Broadway, disenchanted and disillusioned with movies. And, once again, he found his return to the stage very hard going. In October 1932, he appeared in 'I Loved You Wednesday'. The play folded after 63 performances and his next, 'Chrysalis', did even worse, closing after only 23 performances. He was even unluckier with 'Our Wife' at the Booth

Left: Bogart was billed tenth as one of many murder suspects in his second film of 1932, *Big City Blues* (Warner Bros.). With him were Joan Blondell and Eric Linden (back) and Inez Courtney and Ned Sparks (front).

Below: *Three on a Match* (First National-Warner Bros.) was notable for giving Bogart his first gangster role. In this scene are Lyle Talbot, Bogart, Allen Jenkins, Ann Dvorak, Jack La Rue and the young Buster Phelps.

Theater. Only ten people were in the audience for the opening and Bogart – who was on a percentage of the profits – earned only $56 from the show's 20 performances.

The Depression ensured that money was tight and Broadway suffered accordingly. Bogart had a short run in the comedy 'The Mask and the Face', with Shirley Booth, Leo G. Carroll and Judith Anderson, but he and Mary were having a tough time trying to survive. His father was unable to help and once again Bogart was forced to turn to movies to earn enough to live on.

The film was *Midnight* (1934), directed by Chester Erskine for Universal on a miserly budget of $50000 at the Thomas Edison Studios in New York, which had been especially reopened for the production. Bogart had the small part of gangster – a role he was given only when the previously cast actor fell ill.

With no money and no job, Bogart was reduced to playing chess for a dollar a game

17

Above: Bogart's attempts to break through alternately on screen and stage continued when he appeared at the Sam H. Harris Theater in 1932 in 'I Loved You Wednesday' with Rose Hobart. It was another bad failure.

Far right: A desperate Bogart was reduced in the mid-1930s to playing chess against the public for a dollar a game to help him pay his way. This picture is from 1955, when he could enjoy a game without the pressure of needing to win.

against the public in arcades on New York's Sixth Avenue. He was in one of these when he heard that his father was dying and hurried back to his parents' apartment in Tudor City. Two days later, in September 1934, Dr Bogart died in his son's arms, leaving him a ruby ring which Bogart was always to wear. He also left debts of some $10000, which the actor undertook to pay off. Not that, at that particular stage in his life, Bogart could see much chance of fulfilling the obligation.

His luck was due to change, however. First he succeeded in getting a part in the thriller 'Invitation to a Murder' at the Masque Theater, appearing with Gale Sondergaard and Walter Abel. And it was during the play's run that producer Arthur Hopkins and actor Leslie Howard came to see him perform.

'The Petrified Forest' had been written by Robert E. Sherwood while he waited for his divorce to come through in Reno and, sailing the Atlantic on the liner *Majestic* to co-write the film *The Scarlet Pimpernel* for producer

Alexander Korda, he had met its star, Leslie Howard. Howard liked the play and agreed to take the leading role.

By late 1934 the play had almost entirely been cast, with Peggy Conklin, Charles Dow Clarke and Blanche Sweet among the performers selected by producer Hopkins and Howard's partner Gilbert Miller. Only one key role remained unfilled – that of the foul-mouthed and vicious killer Duke Mantee. Sherwood knew Bogart through his friendship with Bill Brady Jr, who had produced his first play 'The Road to Rome' in 1927, and thought he would suit the part of the heroine's footballer beau. But when Hopkins saw Bogart in 'Invitation to a Murder', he knew that he had found his Duke Mantee. Sherwood didn't agree and left the choice to Howard. Howard saw Bogart on stage and sided immediately with Hopkins. Bogart got the part, with Howard insisting.

'The Petrified Forest' marked a milestone in Bogart's career. The play opened in Boston and played there for two weeks, opening on Broadway on 7 January 1935. Leslie Howard was feted by the critics and the play itself was a smash hit. Bogart and Howard became friends and Howard told him that if 'The Petrified Forest' were filmed, he would insist that Bogart repeat his characterization of Duke Mantee. And the play's success enabled Bogart to pay off his and his father's debts.

Warner Brothers bought the screen rights to *The Petrified Forest* and signed Howard to repeat his role. But, since they had plenty of actors – including Edward G. Robinson – under contract who were well versed in playing gangster parts, they saw no reason to give Bogart the role of Duke Mantee. Howard kept his word. He told Warners that unless Bogart was Mantee in the film, he would refuse to make it. Warners capitulated and Bogart was signed for the film – and to a contract with the studio.

Seen today, the film of *The Petrified Forest* (1936) often appears to be both stage-bound and studio-bound and the sets and backdrops of the Arizona Black Mesa Filling Station and Bar-B-Q only add to a general air of unreality. But it is not the settings which give the movie its power, but the drama and characterizations. While the performances, Howard's and Bogart's in particular honed to perfection during their Broadway run, still have resonances of stage drama, the movie's cumulative effect is still undeniably powerful and must have been even more so to contemporary audiences. The story is a mixture of pure melodrama and somewhat pretentious statements about the human condition, the latter largely put over through the relationship between Howard's wandering British

writer and Bette Davis as the waitress trapped in the dreary environment of the Bar-B-Q and dreaming of an escape into the outside world.

Bogart, however, seizes on his role as the gangster holding the occupants of the bar hostage while he waits for the arrival of his girlfriend, and his performance marks a star's appearance in what is, essentially, a supporting role. His Duke Mantee, cold-eyed and unshaven, is a compelling and chilling one, even surviving Sherwood's overwritten introduction (put into the mouth of a fellow gangster): 'This is Duke Mantee, the world-famous killer, and he's hungry.' The characterization remains – for both fans and critics – one of Bogart's best, even though it

was to confine him to many years of playing gangsters and assorted villains on the screen.

Critically, Bogart fared well with *The Petrified Forest*: the *Monthly Film Bulletin* said: 'Where all are so good it is almost invidious to name individuals but mention must be made of a remarkable performance by Humphrey Bogart . . .' while *Film Weekly* claimed: 'Bogart's study of Duke Mantee, the killer, is a remarkable piece of acting, underlining without exaggeration the animal-like mentality of a professional murderer . . .' And the *New York Times* reviewer noted: 'There should be a large measure of praise for Humphrey Bogart . . . who can be a psychopathic gangster more like Dillinger than the outlaw himself',

Bogart finally arrived when he made *The Petrified Forest* (Warner Bros.) with Bette Davis and Leslie Howard. As Duke Mantee, a killer, he was triumphant, and his screen success was assured.

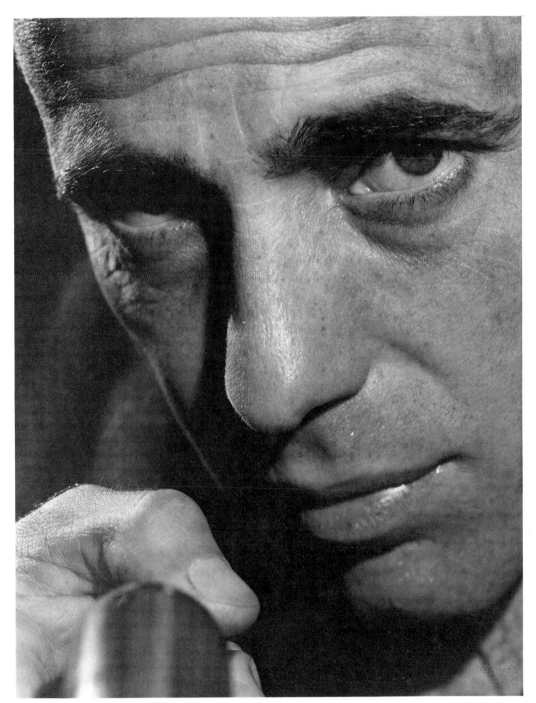

The gangster image which set the pattern for most of Bogart's earliest successes, and established the character of a self-sufficient loner which he was to play convincingly in many guises.

while for *Picturegoer*: 'Humphrey Bogart . . . acts with such understanding that one pities the man as much as one detests the crime he commits.'

Nearly two decades later, Bogart played Mantee again, in a live television production directed by Delbert Mann, with Henry Fonda in the role originally essayed by Howard and with Bogart's wife in the Bette Davis part. He was still triumphantly in command and the *New York Times* wrote: 'Last night, in what was his debut on a live TV drama, he was cold, vicious and convincingly peremptory. Few actors can suggest so much evil so quietly.'

Bogart's third attempt to crack Hollywood was a major triumph. This time there would be no return to Broadway in search of stage work. In *The Petrified Forest* he had shown that he possessed the one great attribute that would make him a star – sheer screen presence and charisma of a sort that immediately won him empathy from audiences.

He had a Warner Brothers contract that paid him $650 a week and even if he was to have to wait for *High Sierra* in 1941 to achieve real stardom, Bogart the star was at least on his way. Bogart, the legend, would follow.

GANGSTERS AND THE BATTLING BOGARTS

Bogart's success in *The Petrified Forest* ensured that he no longer had to worry about being cast as callow juveniles. But, as he served out his contract at Warner Brothers, it soon became clear that the film had put him into another area of typecasting.

He was later to be quoted as saying: 'In my first 34 films I was shot in 12, electrocuted or hanged in eight, and was a jailbird in nine. I was the Little Lord Fauntleroy of the lot.'

Inevitably, it seemed, Bogart was to be confined to playing gangsters and heavies as part of Warner Brothers' line-up of gangster actors. The studio had pioneered the gangster film and, in so doing, had put together a group of notable performers in the genre, known locally as Murderer's Row. Bogart found himself joining such villainous stalwarts as James Cagney, George Raft, Edward G. Robinson, Paul Muni and John Garfield. He also found that he was the low man on the totem pole when it came to being assigned parts by the studio, and he was soon in fairly constant conflict with Jack L. Warner in an attempt to be given better parts.

However, he was well aware of the need to confine his rebellion and not to follow Bette Davis and other Warner stars into suspension. He said: 'I'm known as the guy who always squawks about roles, but never refuses to play one. I've never forgotten a piece of advice Holbrook Blinn gave me when I was a young squirt and I asked him how I could get a reputation as an actor. He said: "Just keep working". The idea is that if you're always busy, sometime somebody is going to get the idea that you must be good.'

He certainly followed that advice, making 28 movies between *The Petrified Forest* and ultimate stardom with *High Sierra*. His first was a remake of *Five Star Final*, now titled *Two against the World*. Bogart was the lead, the setting was changed to a radio station and William McGann directed with pace but little flair. It was forgettable and Bogart chose to do just that.

It was followed by *Bullets or Ballots*, made before *Two against the World* (1936) but released shortly afterwards. The crime melodrama was directed by William Keighley who moved things along at a cracking pace, coming up with a film that pleased both the fans and the critics. Edward G. Robinson had the lead, playing a cop who was working undercover as a gangster, and Bogart was a trigger-happy genuine gangster in the employ of villain Barton MacLane. This was one of the movies in which Bogart was shot. *The Observer* noted: 'Mr Bogart is a most successful tough guy and I should say the chances are entirely remote that he will ever be allowed to play a law-abiding citizen again.'

In fact, his next film featured him as a First World War airman united with Pat O'Brien in starting up an airline across the Pacific. *China Clipper* (1936) was simply a programmer – and looked it. In *Isle of Fury* (1936) he was cast as a fugitive holed up on a South Seas island, and the tepid novel by Somerset Maugham on which it was based turned out even more lifeless in the screenplay by Robert Andrews and William Jacobs. The *Monthly Film Bulletin* thought the film lack-

Edward G. Robinson was already an established Warner Brothers gangster when Bogart first graced the genre, and the two played together in *Bullets or Ballots*, in which Bogart was a racketeer and Robinson this time an undercover cop.

Left: Bogart appeared with a moustache in *Isle of Fury* (Warner Bros.), based on Somerset Maugham's story. He was a fugitive who reformed. E. E. Clive, Donald Woods and Margaret Lindsay are with him in this scene.

ing in coherence, but praised Bogart's performance in making his character credible. He teamed up again with Pat O'Brien for 1937's *The Great O'Malley* as a man who turns to crime to support his crippled daughter. O'Brien played a cop and the resulting film was a sickly confection. 'It was', claimed Bogart, 'terrible, but it was one of those things we did at that goddamned sweatshop. Pat was very good. Pat was never bad.'

Black Legion (1937) was well received critically and many thought it was Bogart's best film up to that time – not, however, a judgement with which he agreed, since he still preferred *The Petrified Forest*. He was an American factory worker who becomes involved with a secret organization similar to the Ku Klux Klan. This one saw him ending up in prison. The movie was described by the *New York Herald Tribune* as 'outstanding and memorable' and *The Observer* critic wrote: 'The film is obviously one of Warner Brothers films with a mission . . . so seriously played and so hotly argued that nobody can miss the point, but not everybody, I'm afraid, will share the passion.' And *Film Weekly* said of the star: 'Bogart gives a magnificent performance. He wins sympathy for the character but never whitewashes it, or even deliberately plays on one's feelings.'

By now, Bogart was well established in Hollywood. He was already notable for his cheerful refusal to comply with what was demanded of movie stars. The Hollywood establishment and their ways left him cold. He was disinterested in the popular art of

Sent to jail for a minor offence, Bogart escapes and nearly kills the cop who jailed him in *The Great O'Malley* (Warner Bros.). Bogart admired co-star Pat O'Brien, but hated the film.

image building and would not allow studio publicists to photograph him in the kind of unbelievable off-screen poses that were popular at the time. Indeed, off-screen, Bogart tended to be the same cynical and hard-boiled character that he was often playing for Warner Brothers. He told one fan magazine in 1937 that: 'I believe in speaking my mind. I don't believe in hiding anything. If you're ashamed of anything, correct it. There's nothing I won't talk about.' And, in subsequent interviews, he proved to be true

Right: *Marked Woman*
(Warner Bros.) featured
Bogart as a District Attorney.
The four women with him
here are Rosalind Marquis,
Mayo Methot, Lola Lane and
Bette Davis. Bogart married
Mayo Methot, his third wife,
during the making of the film.

Below: Bogart and second
wife Mary Phillips in their
apartment in 1936. She caught
him there with Mayo Methot,
and filed for divorce, Bogart
marrying Methot soon
afterwards.

to his word. He was quoted as saying 'All
over Hollywood they are continually advis-
ing me "Oh, you mustn't say that. That'll
get you in a lot of trouble", when I remark
that some picture or director or writer or
producer is no good. I don't get it. If he or
it isn't any good, why can't you say so? If
more people would mention it, pretty soon
it might have some effect. This local idea that
anyone making a thousand dollars a week is
sacred and beyond the realm of criticism
never strikes me as particularly sound
reasoning.'

If Bogart generally despised the mores of
the Hollywood establishment and never
failed to take opportunities to express his
distinctly cynical view of the place, he was
particularly contemptuous of the continuing
string of villainous roles – and second-league
ones at that – being handed him by Warner
Brothers. Unfortunately, Jack L. Warner
was perfectly happy to see Bogart continue
to make more of the same kind of movies,
claiming to Bogart that: 'Nothing can happen to your face that will hurt it a bit.'

Bogart also told an interviewer in 1937:
'I believe in the institution of marriage. The
institution is right, it's the human beings
who are wrong. I believe in love, but not
"the one love of a lifetime", as pretty a tale
as that always makes. There couldn't be just
one love – among 50 million people, that
would be pretty hard to find. Love is very
warming, heartening, enjoyable, a necessary

exercise for the heart and soul and intelligence. It you're not in love, you dry up. I am in love now. After all, the best proof a man can give of his belief in love and marriage is to marry more than once.'

He was about to prove that he stood by his words on the subject. His second marriage was going far from smoothly. Mary had come out to Hollywood with her husband, but soon became increasingly bored with her enforced inactivity. Bogart was constantly working while she had nothing to do but pass the time in their Garden of Allah apartment.

When she decided to accept a leading role back on Broadway in 'The Postman Always Rings Twice', Bogart was angered but was unable to prevent her from leaving for New York. But he soon found consolation.

He had been cast as a tough District Attorney determined to persuade Bette Davis and her fellow nightclub hostesses to testify against their gangster boss Eduardo Cinaelli in *Marked Woman* (1937). The movie, a courtroom melodrama briskly directed by Lloyd Bacon, was greeted by *Variety* as: '. . . a strong, well-made underworld drama' but, for Bogart, the drama was all off-screen.

Marked Woman featured a tough, hard-drinking blonde, Mayo Methot, as one of the hostesses, and Bogart, who had known her in New York, soon found himself involved in an affair with her. She moved in with him into the apartment at the Garden of Allah and his second marriage was finally over when Mary, on a quick trip back from New York, caught them there together. She returned to New York to file for divorce and Bogart found himself trapped into a third marriage. It was to be one that was stormy, even by Hollywood standards.

Bogart laid out the ground rules for the marriage in another interview, saying: 'Another reason why we get on so well together is that we don't have illusions about each other. We know just what we're getting, so there can't be any complaints on that score after we're married. Illusions are no good in marriage. And I love a good fight. So does Mayo. We have some first-class battles.'

Bogart told no less than the truth and their battles were really first-class ones – even by Hollywood standards – and often took place in public with a total lack of inhibitions. The couple were married in Beverly Hills on 20 August 1938 and, allegedly, Bogart spent his wedding night alone after a swinging row with Mayo. On their New York honeymoon at the Algonquin Hotel, one of their fights resulted in a $400 bill for damage to their room, and the battles continued unabated on their return to the Hollywood house Bogart had bought on Horn Avenue.

It did not take long for the pair to become known as 'The Battling Bogarts' and Bogart and Mayo – whom he nicknamed 'Sluggy' – never failed to maintain their warring reputation. Mayo was a hard and heavy drinker and soon Bogart's consumption of alcohol rose to keep pace with her's. Although he was never to match her, he became a hard drinker, claiming that what was wrong with the world was that everyone in it was always permanently three drinks below a level he considered to be the right one.

Their constant fights became headline material. After all, Bogart was only confirming in real life the image he had been given as a tough, two-fisted man of action in all his roles in movies. On one occasion, Mayo stabbed him in the back. On another, she threw a soda-water bottle at him, only just missing him and causing Bogart to take out a huge life-insurance policy against a time when her aim might improve. On yet a further occasion, Bogart rang the Warner Brothers publicity department to announce – from inside his locked bathroom – that Mayo was threatening to shoot him. The

Bogart and Methot on a porch of their Hollywood home. The door in the foreground was kept locked, as the pair preferred to use a side entrance.

incident ended with Mayo firing a shot through his suitcase instead of through him.

All the publicity engendered by these incidents simply served to enhance Bogart's popular image, on and off the screen, and it also led to assorted members of the public attempting to call him out to justify his tough-guy persona. But, once, it was Mayo who slugged the would-be hero, earning Bogart's unstinted admiration.

Warner Brothers, immensely pleased at the fortune his movies were making for them, kept Bogart hard at work. Before *Marked Woman* and his marriage, he had appeared in *San Quentin* (1937), playing a convict, with Pat O'Brien as a prison warden, and earning for himself the comment from *Film Weekly* that: 'Humphrey Bogart, as usual, makes a sympathetic and impressive figure of the tough "Red".' Since he was involved in a marriage whose brawls would have floored a lesser man, it says much for Bogart's sheer professionalism – to say nothing of his stamina – that he went right on working.

Under director William Wyler for *Dead End* (United Artists), Bogart became a gangster again and made one of his best films of the 1930s.

Kid Galahad (1937)· co-starred him with Edward G. Robinson, the two of them playing rival boxing managers, and he made *Dead End* (1937) on loan to Samuel Goldwyn, turning in a first-rate performance streets ahead of his Warner Brothers films under William Wyler's direction. The film was a savage indictment of the punishing life in the New York slums, with Bogart playing a vicious killer, probably his best role since Duke Mantee, and proving to be a deeply moving actor in a small scene with Claire Trevor, who played his mother. The film introduced the Dead End Kids and emerged as a powerful – now dated – sociological drama with *Film Weekly* commenting: 'In Bogart's brilliant characterization there is plain crime and the odd psychology of the killer.' And his next picture – his first comedy – was also made outside Warners, by Walter Wanger in conjunction with United Artists, casting Bogart as a hard-drinking film studio production chief and reuniting him with Leslie Howard and Joan Blondell in 1937's *Stand-In*. Said *The Cinema*: 'Humphrey Bogart runs Leslie Howard a close second for honours with his interesting, sincere and truthful portrait of a good producer too easily swayed by his emotions.'

It was back to Warners for 1938's *Swing Your Lady*, a dire backwoods farce which had Bogart as a wrestling promoter. He was later to claim that this was the worst film he made and the *Monthly Film Bulletin* felt, rightly, that it was a waste of his talents.

Although his marriage continued on its hard-hitting course with little let-up, Mayo was not always the complete battling near-alcoholic. She made her husband employ a first-rate business manager, Morgan Maree, who looked after his finances, and also organized the funeral of his mother – who had come to live with the couple – when she died of cancer aged 75.

But Bogart had little time in which to assess leisurely the progress of his marriage. *Men Are Such Fools* (1938) was directed improbably by Busby Berkeley, better known as a director of lavish musicals, and was terrible. It was likely that Warner Brothers, having finally succumbed to Bogart's pressure for more money, were taking it out on him by putting him into the worst pictures they could find, although *Crime School* (1938) was marginally better, with Bogart playing a reform school warden busy reforming the Dead End Kids and earning from *Film Weekly* the comment that he was 'efficient, restrained and completely effective as always'. He hated *The Amazing Dr Clitterhouse* (1938), in which he played the gangster boss of a gang of jewel thieves along with Edward G. Robinson, and would vul-

garly refer to it as 'The Amazing Dr Clitoris'.

Racket Busters (1938) was simply another 'B' picture crime thriller with Bogart efficient as ever as a gangster running a protection racket against New York truckers. *Angels with Dirty Faces* (1938) was yet another of the seemingly endless series of Warner's crime films, with Bogart, playing one more gangster, losing out in the acting stakes to James Cagney's killer, persuaded by prison priest Pat O'Brien into pretending to be a coward as he goes to the electric chair in order to deter the Dead End Kids (again!) from embarking on a life of crime. Michael Curtiz, Warner's workhorse contract director, kept the proceedings moving along briskly and the movie has a treasured place in the Bogart canon among afficionados. The 'Cinematograph Exhibitors' Association of Great Britain and Ireland Film Report' said of the film that: 'Those who like their entertainment without frills will enjoy the picture', adding: 'Humphrey Bogart and George Bancroft are well cast and convincing racketeers . . .' Bogart found himself in more of the same with the first of his seven

27

1939 pictures, *King of the Underworld*: he was killed yet again as hoodlum Joe Gurney.

He was shot once more, this time by James Cagney, in his second Western, 1939's *The Oklahoma Kid*. The film simply served to prove that cowboys were not Bogart's metier. The three-hankie weepie *Dark Victory* (1939) had him playing an Irish race-horse trainer and appearing with President-to-be Ronald Reagan, but the movie belonged firmly to star Bette Davis while *You Can't Get Away with Murder* (1939) showed Warner Brothers doing just that by casting him yet again as a gangster involved with Dead End Kid Billy Halop. Way down in the cast list of *Invisible Stripes* (1939) was another Dead End Kid, Leo Gorcey, Bogart playing another gangster in a movie that he hated. He died again in 1939's *The Roaring Twenties*, a story of gangsterism and mayhem in Prohibition days, co-starring James Cagney. The story was strong and the film was a good one, but for Bogart, it must have seemed like one more assignment off the assembly line. His last 1939 picture marked the nadir of the stories handed to him by Warner Brothers. In *The Return of Dr X*, a 'B' picture horror movie, Bogart was a vampire newly returned from the dead with a white stripe in his hair and a neat line in pin-stripe suits. 'This', Bogart told an interviewer, 'was one of the pictures that made

King of the Underworld (Warner Bros.) was beginning to be a good description of Bogart's screen persona in the late 1930s. This publicity portrait for the film captures the menace he conveyed around this time.

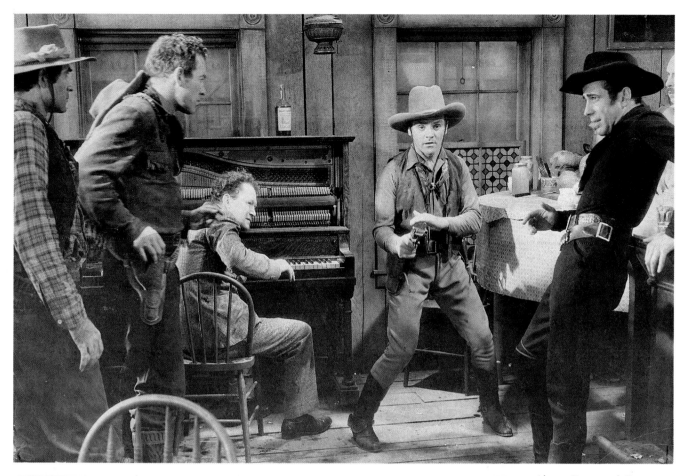

Above: Bogart and Cagney
together again in a Western,
The Oklahoma Kid (Warner
Bros.), in which Bogart
unconvincingly led an outlaw
gang.

Left: George Raft was another
of Warner Brothers' stable of
gangsters in the 1930s, and he
and Bogart both met sticky
ends as gang colleagues in
Invisible Stripes.

The Roaring Twenties (Warner Bros.) was a film about strife between racketeers during the days of Prohibition. Bogart, Cagney and Jeffrey Lynn were war buddies who took to the liquor-running business and destroyed each other.

me march in to Jack Warner and ask for more money again. You can't believe what this one was like. I had a part that somebody like Bela Lugosi or Boris Karloff should have played. I was this doctor, brought back to life, and the only thing that nourished this poor bastard was blood. If it'd been Jack Warner's blood, or Harry's, or Pop's, maybe I wouldn't have minded as much. The

trouble was, they were drinking mine and I was making this stinking movie.'

The year 1940 started no more auspiciously with his third Western, *Virginia City*, in which, wearing an unattractive moustache, he was killed by star Errol Flynn, a man admired by Bogart for his legendary drinking capabilities, if nothing else. *Virginia City* was followed by *It All Came True* (1940), an alleged comedy with Bogart as a gangster on the run holing up in the boarding house run by Una O'Connor and Jessie Busley. It did nothing for his career. Neither did his final 1940 picture *Brother Orchid*, in which the acting honours went to Edward G. Robinson as a gangster turned monk, with Bogart as a hoodlum who sticks to his chosen profession, although the satire earned from *The Times* the comment: 'Mr Humphrey Bogart gives another of his smooth, cold exercises in villainy . . .' They were exercises that, by now, he could easily have performed in his sleep. His career could hardly have been much busier – but it could not, it appeared, have been less likely to bring him the stardom presaged by *The Petrified Forest*.

Ironically, it was through his co-star in his first 1941 movie, *They Drive by Night*, that Bogart finally got the break that took him to the top. The movie had Bogart playing George Raft's younger brother in a tough, pacy and thoroughly enjoyable melodrama about truckers taking on their crooked bosses. The dialogue was sharp and the movie was a typically polished production by Mark Hellinger, the journalist-turned-producer who had introduced Bogart to the pleasure of Scotch, and Raoul Walsh's direction was his usual efficient, if anonymous, piece of work.

Right: Bogart was George Raft's brother in *They Drive by Night* (Warner Bros.), an exciting story about corruption in the trucking business. Ann Sheridan helped the brothers fight the crooks attempting to control the truckers.

HERE'S LOOKING AT YOU, KID

George Raft was one of Warner Brothers' first string of screen gangsters, along with James Cagney, Edward G. Robinson, John Garfield and Paul Muni and, as such, was always given first go at the plum movie assignments.

The gangster in *High Sierra* (1941) had to die at the end of the film at the dictates of the censors. Offered the part, Raft turned it down, refusing to expire. James Cagney followed suit and so, in rapid succession, did Paul Muni (who was offended that it had been offered to others before him), and Edward G. Robinson. So Bogart got the part that was to make him a star at 41, simply because Warners had run out of anyone else to cast as Roy Earle.

On paper, the movie, which had Bogart as a big-time gangster who is sprung from jail to pull off a hotel hold-up, becomes romantically involved with a crippled girl and ends up in a fatal gunfight with the police high up in the mountains, must have looked like just another run-of-the-bullet gangster melodrama. In Bogart's hands, it turned into a crime classic, forcing the studio finally to acknowledge that he was a star. Every aspect of the movie coalesces. The script is taut, spare and laconic, Raoul Walsh's direction exemplary and the supporting cast, led by Ida Lupino, is impeccable.

But the film belongs totally to Bogart's superbly developed characterization of Roy Earle. Despite its heavy maudlin elements (his affection for the crippled girl and his paying for her to have her club foot operated on, and his final death because he refuses to abandon a stray dog), the script gave Bogart the opportunity to give a totally rounded performance and to show the man behind the vicious killer. He succeeded in making Mad Dog Roy Earle both credible and sym-

Close-up of a scene being shot for *High Sierra* (Warner Bros.). Bogart gives road directions to Henry Travers and Elizabeth Risdon (in car) in a role which he was lucky to get, but which confirmed his status as a star.

HIGH SIERRA

with
ALAN CURTIS · ARTHUR KENNEDY
JOAN LESLIE · HENRY HULL · HENRY TRAVERS

Directed by
RAOUL WALSH
SCREEN PLAY BY JOHN HUSTON and W. R. BURNETT · FROM A NOVEL BY W. R. BURNETT
A WARNER BROS. — FIRST NATIONAL PICTURE

Presented by
WARNER BROS.

starring
IDA
LUPINO
HUMPHREY
BOGART

Star billing for Bogart in a film which was to be a critical triumph for him. He played an escaped killer who teams up with Ida Lupino, and captures the sympathy of the audience before his statutory death at the end.

pathetic. He dominated the picture and both public and critics liked what they saw.

'One of the very few actors who can communicate a sinister physical presence', said *The Sunday Times* of Bogart, 'dominating' asserted the *Monthly Film Bulletin*, while for *Today's Cinema*: 'Bogart dwarfed everyone else in the cast.' The *New York Herald Tribune* critic wrote: 'Humphrey Bogart was the perfect choice to play the role. Always a fine actor, he is particularly splendid as a farm

boy turned outlaw, who is shocked and hurt when newspapers refer to him as a mad dog. His steady portrayal is what makes this melodrama more than merely exciting.'

Warners, now well aware that they had a star – although hardly a new one – on their hands, gave him top billing for the first time in 1941's *The Wagons Roll at Night*, a routine movie directed by routine director Ray Enright and casting him as the boss of a travelling circus. He was good as usual, but the picture was simply another pot-boiler.

Bogart's stardom was triumphantly confirmed with his next film, however, and *The Maltese Falcon* (1941) is, for many, his finest and most thoroughly enjoyable picture. And, once again he had George Raft to thank for the break.

The Maltese Falcon was to be screen writer John Huston's first directorial assignment and, when he was offered the role of private eye Sam Spade, Raft turned it down since he was not about to entrust his career to a tyro director. It must have been galling for him when not only did the film emerge as an all-time classic thriller that established Bogart as the quintessential private detective, but it was also nominated for an Oscar as Best Picture.

Dashiell Hammett's novel had been filmed twice before, once as *The Maltese Falcon* in 1931 with Ricardo Cortez in the lead and again, as *Satan Met a Lady* in 1936, with Warren William as Sam Spade. This time writer-director Huston (who had co-scripted *High Sierra*), returned to Hammett's novel, coming up with a complex, fascinating and suave concoction of murder and mystery as Bogart's Sam Spade became caught up in the search for a fabulous jewel-encrusted statuette, with ambivalent *femme fatale* Mary Astor and the memorable villainy of crooks Sydney Greenstreet, Peter Lorre and Elisha Cook Jr.

Made on a budget of only $300 000, the movie was brilliantly directed and written by Huston, superbly photographed by Arthur Edeson, and the whole cast gave flawless performances, dominated by Bogart's laconic detective. He succeeded in showing the ambiguous man behind the tough wisecracking façade of Sam Spade, a moral man in the tradition of Raymond Chandler's Philip Marlowe, whom he was to play in 1946's superb *The Big Sleep*. Clearly, in this, the first of the five films Bogart was to make with Huston, the two had complete empathy and were to become firm friends.

When *The Maltese Falcon* was released, it became an instant favourite with filmgoers, and critical acclaim was equally strong. *Kine Weekly* averred: 'Bogart is brilliant as the unethical Spade', having previously com-

A publicity shot of Bogart issued for *The Maltese Falcon* (Warner Bros.) in which he was superbly directed by John Huston, making his debut as a director.

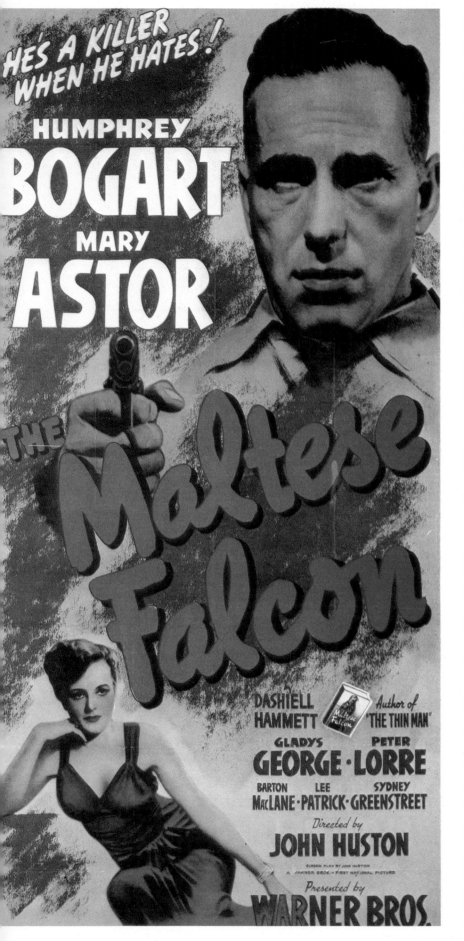

HE'S A KILLER WHEN HE HATES!

HUMPHREY
BOGART

MARY
ASTOR

THE Maltese Falcon

DASHIELL HAMMETT — Author of 'THE THIN MAN'

GLADYS
GEORGE · PETER
LORRE

BARTON
MacLANE · LEE
PATRICK · SYDNEY
GREENSTREET

Directed by
JOHN HUSTON

Screen Play by John Huston
A Warner Bros. - First National Picture

Presented by
WARNER BROS.

mented on its 'brilliant characterization, resourceful direction and imaginative camerawork . . .' *The New York Times* said: 'The trick which Mr Huston has pulled is a combination of American ruggedness with the suavity of the English crime school – a blend of mind and muscle – plus a slight touch of pathos', while the *New Statesman* commented: '*The Maltese Falcon* has nearly everything a mystery film should have.' *Sight and Sound* called it: 'The best thriller so far this year' and *The Sunday Times* thought it: 'The most interesting and imaginative detective film to come out of America, or anywhere else, since the first *Thin Man*, another Hammett story. Bogart is as good as he can be. The defensive, admiring and calculating stare on his first encounter with the beauty, the physical self-confidence he puts into their later meetings, his resentful, implacable rejection of her appeal at the last – who could do these scenes better, or as well?'

Bogart followed *The Maltese Falcon* with 1942's *All Through the Night*, a propaganda piece that is now very dated as, still a gangster but this time a patriotic one with his heart firmly in the right place, he took on Nazis Conrad Veidt and Peter Lorre. The comedy-thriller won from *Daily Film Renter* the comment that: 'Bogart is naturally superior to his material.' 'So', one might ask oneself, 'what else is new?'

The Big Shot (1942) was a routine gangster picture. Bogart again transcended his material, but it is hard to see why he bothered.

He was reunited with John Huston for *Across the Pacific* (1942) in which, in a slackly scripted movie, he, Huston, Mary Astor and Sydney Greenstreet enjoyed themselves immensely making the story of Bogart foiling Greenstreet's dastardly scheme to help the Japanese war effort by blowing up the Suez Canal. Despite the deliberate re-teaming of *The Maltese Falcon* stars, the movie, although enjoyable, was not as much fun. Vincent Sherman had the unenviable task of wrapping up the movie – whose ending had yet to be convincingly worked out – after Huston had been called up for military service. Said the 'Cinematograph Exhibitors' Association of Great Britain and Ireland Film Report': 'Clever direction and fine character-featuring lift this picture above the average espionage drama . . . Humphrey Bogart is an arresting hero . . .' and *The New York Times* stated that it 'was like having a knife at your ribs for an hour and a half.'

Although fan reaction had long since proved that Bogart was a draw with women as well as men, who reacted to his tough portrayals, it took his next picture, *Casablanca* (1942) totally to show the studio that he was not only true star material but also

a real romantic idol. *Casablanca*, despite its melodramatic trimmings, stands out as a true cinema classic and not simply one of Bogart's greatest pictures, and it is one of the very small number of films which reward constant viewing and re-viewing. It also serves to encapsulate all that is best in the movies that emerged, not from some auteur-director ideal so beloved of intellectual film critics, but from the Hollywood studio system at its peak.

The script for *Casablanca*, by Julius J. and Philip G. Epstein and Howard Koch, was based on the play 'Everybody Comes to Rick's' by Murray Burnett and Joan Alison. Bogart was the eponymous Rick (although few people outside dedicated Bogart buffs can give the character his full name – Richard Blaine), the cynical, world-weary but ultimately gallant and sentimental owner of Rick's Café Americaine in neutral Casablanca during the Second World War, an atmospheric bar-cum-nightclub that served

as a meeting point for every refugee and criminal in the city. The story itself resembled yet another of the Warners' melodramas taken from contemporary headlines, as Bogart met up with old flame Ingrid Bergman, rekindled their romance and then selflessly helped her and her resistance leader husband Paul Henreid to escape from the Nazis, led by Conrad Veidt, and from Claude Rains' venal but likable police official.

During the making of the picture Bogart, Bergman and director Michael Curtiz claimed not to understand what the film was about and to believe that it would turn out disastrously. In the event, it did not and it emerged as one of those rare pictures in which every single aspect comes together perfectly. The casting was impeccable – in addition to Bogart, Bergman, Veidt, Rains and Henreid, Sydney Greenstreet, Peter Lorre and S. Z. Sakall contributed memorable performances, while Dooley Wilson, playing and singing 'As Time Goes By',

Above: The four main protagonists in *The Maltese Falcon* (Warner Bros.), Humphrey Bogart, Peter Lorre, Mary Astor and Sidney Greenstreet, all gave first-class performances, and the film has become one of Bogart's most often re-shown classics.

Far left: Poster for *The Maltese Falcon* (Warner Bros.) in which Bogart played Dashiell Hammett's famous private eye Sam Spade, and played him to perfection.

Bogart was once again the dominating character in *Casablanca* (Warner Bros.), but Dooley Wilson, as the Sam whom Bogart ordered to 'Play it', earned himself a niche in movie legend with his playing and singing of the theme song 'As Time Goes By'.

earned himself a peculiar place as the immortal Sam in movie history.

But Bogart himself towered above everything and everyone else in the film, depicting a man of honour, flawed by stubbornness and self-centredness and made heroic (although the character is, in essence, a genuine anti-hero) by his refusal to compromise. And he proved himself, in his love scenes with Ingrid Bergman (Here's looking at you, kid), to be a true romantic performer.

Casablanca is assured a place high in the Bogart canon. His performance is the one most aped by impersonators and has been used on television by look-alikes to increase sales of such products as alcohol – a point that would no doubt have delighted Bogart. Countless mimics have attempted to lisp (inaccurately, as anyone who knows the film will realize) 'Play it again, Tham.' All these imitators, however, simply end up as just that – imitators. Like all true originals, Bogart is incapable of accurate impersonation.

Bogart received a well-deserved Oscar nomination for *Casablanca*, but Paul Lukas picked it up for his performance in *Watch on the Rhine*. The film won Oscars for Best Picture, Best Screenplay and, for Michael Curtiz, Best Director.

Public acclaim was echoed by critical approval. *Picture Show* said: 'A drama of realism and romance in which their two forces perfectly merge', and, for *The Guardian*, the film was 'bulging with acting talent and breathless with warm, dramatic momentum.' The *Daily Film Renter* said that it was: 'Brilliantly acted by Bogart and a handpicked – not to say extravagantly used – bunch of supporting players, it never wavers in interest and suspense', while, for *The Cinema* it was: 'One of the most arresting instances of political melodrama seen for many a day . . . Bogart strides off with all the acting honours.'

Bogart's marriage was rapidly disintegrating. Mayo was well on the way to becoming

BOGART · BERGMAN · HENREID

Presented by
WARNER BROS.

"Casablanca"

A HAL B. WALLIS PRODUCTION

CLAUDE RAINS · CONRAD VEIDT · SYDNEY GREENSTREET · PETER LORRE

Directed by MICHAEL CURTIZ

SCREEN PLAY BY JULIUS J. & PHILIP G. EPSTEIN and HOWARD KOCH · FROM A PLAY BY MURRAY BURNETT and JOAN ALISON
MUSIC BY MAX STEINER · A WARNER BROS.—FIRST NATIONAL PICTURE

Above: Poster for the Oscar-winning *Casablanca* (Warner Bros.), one of the most popular films of all time, in which Bogart convincingly played an unconventional romantic lead opposite Ingrid Bergman.

Left: Bogart as the owner of Rick's, a gin palace in *Casablanca* (Warner Bros.), to which resistance leader Paul Henreid and his wife, Bogart's ex-flame Ingrid Bergman, flee to escape the Germans in the Second World War. Claude Rains was a devious police chief.

an alcoholic and, on the set of *Casablanca*, she triggered off more brawls with her husband whom, she was convinced, was in love with Ingrid Bergman. And, after the success of the film at the Academy Awards ceremony, she attempted to kill herself. Bogart persuaded her to see a psychiatrist, who confirmed that she was now a complete alcoholic and a paranoid schizophrenic. But, despite his and Bogart's urging, she refused psychiatric treatment.

Bogart had negotiated a new seven-year contract with Warner Brothers just before making *Casablanca*, giving him $3 500 a week for 40 weeks work every year and the studio had no options: the contract was valid for as long as Bogart chose to honour it.

Following *Casablanca*, Bogart starred with Raymond Massey in a rousing propa-ganda piece *Action· in the North Atlantic* (1943). They played fellow officers in a tribute to the wartime merchant marine and the film moved at a cracking pace under Lloyd Bacon's direction, aided by excellent special effects. During its making, Bogart and Massey got into an argument as to whose stand-in was the toughest. In order to settle it, to the director's horror, they dumped the doubles and jumped from the bridge of a burning ship into the fire-covered water.

Still fighting, Bogart and Mayo left for Europe and a USO tour in Europe and Africa around Christmas 1943, bringing a powerful dose of hand-to-hand conflict to the already war-torn battle zones. The marriage was over in all but name. They entertained the troops together, Bogart with speeches from his films, beginning with one

Bogart's successful pairing with Ingrid Bergman in *Casablanca* caused him more trouble with his wife Mayo Methot and hastened the break-up of an already disintegrating marriage.

from *The Petrified Forest*, and Mayo singing to the accordion of Don Cummings.

On their return to Hollywood, the two continued to fight but, at least, he was now, after the reaction to *Casablanca* and his Oscar nomination, Warner's top star and king of the lot. His next picture, however, was for Columbia and was directed by Zoltan Korda with plenty of action and entertainment value as Bogart led a bunch of assorted soldiers against the Germans during the retreat from Tobruk. *Sahara* (1943) earned from *Time* magazine the comment: 'This story is told so expertly, detail by detail, that the whole unlikely affair seems believable. More than that – it often approximates hard and honest facts about war and about people. *Sahara* rings dozens of changes on old formulas, and in their simple way, they make more hard sense pictorially than most documentaries. Humphrey Bogart is the only well-known actor in the picture. To say that he is as good as the rest of the cast is high praise.' The rest of the cast included Dan Duryea, J. Carrol Naish, Lloyd Bridges, Rex Ingram and Bruce Bennett.

After a brief appearance in Warner Brothers' all-star musical revue *Thank Your Lucky Stars* (1943) – in which he parodied his gangster persona – Bogart went into a dismal little thriller, *Conflict*, in which he played a wife-killer. Sidney Greenstreet was in this one and he and Bogart appeared together for the last time in *Passage to Marseille*, another of the studio's contributions to the war effort, depicting a group of prisoners escaping from Devil's Island to help France to fight the Germans. Trying to prove that imitation was the sincerest form of box-office insurance, the film also featured *Casablanca* co-stars Claude Rains and Peter Lorre and was directed by Michael Curtiz. But the resemblance ended there. *Passage to Marseille* was a mediocre movie, despite its starry cast.

If Mayo's outbursts during the making of *Casablanca* and afterwards had registered the final disintegration of her marriage to Bogart, his next picture, 1945's *To Have and Have Not* finally spelled the end to the turbulent and unhappy relationship. For Bogart's leading lady in the picture, making her first film, was Lauren Bacall.

Passage to Marseille (Warner Bros.) was an attempt to re-create some of the atmosphere of *Casablanca*, and had Bogart (centre, rear) playing an escapee from Devil's Island who prevents a French ship being taken over by Fascists. The picture failed.

BETTY BACALL

Far right: Lauren Bacall had met Bogart briefly before she made her film debut opposite him in *To Have and Have Not*. She became his fourth wife.

The movie *To Have and Have Not* was clearly designed to repeat the formula – and the box-office success – of *Casablanca*, right down to Bogart's role which turned out to be a near reprise of Rick. He was the cynical American expatriate Harry Morgan, the skipper of a charter boat in Martinique and not above the occasional bit of gun-running, who reluctantly becomes involved in the efforts of the underground movement against the Vichy French and the Germans. *The Guardian* noted the similarity between the two pictures, commenting: 'Results are above average, especially for those who never saw *Casablanca*, a slightly better edition of the same story.'

The story, in fact, had its genesis in a private bet between producer-director Howard Hawks and Ernest Hemingway. Hawks had claimed that he could make a good movie from anything written by Hemingway and the writer had retaliated with *To Have and Have Not*, clearly forgetting about Hollywood's notorious way with any original story material. By the time Hawks and his two writers – Jules Furthman and William Faulkner – had finished, there was practically no Hemingway but a great deal of Hollywood. (Hemingway's original story was more faithfully filmed by Michael Curtiz in 1950 as *The Breaking Point*, while 1958's *The Gun Runners* starred Audie Murphy in a reworking of the Bogart role). For *To Have and Have Not*, Hemingway's original locale of Florida and Cuba was altered – at the request of Nelson Rockefeller's American Affairs Committee – to Martinique in order not to offend Latin-American sensitivities, and the Cuban villains became Vichy Frenchmen.

Bogart's leading lady was making her screen debut in *To Have and Have Not*. Born Betty Perske in New York on 16 September 1924, she had had a brief career as an actress and model and had been noticed on the cover of the February 1943 edition of *Harper's Bazaar* by Hawks' wife Nancy. Hawks gave her a screen test. While it was clear that her acting ability was limited, he could see potential and she was undoubtedly superbly photogenic. Hawks signed her up to a personal seven-year contract, shared with Warner Brothers, at $250 a week. Betty Perske had already changed her name to Betty Bacall. Hawks substituted Lauren but Bacall was always to prefer to be called Betty.

She first met Bogart briefly on the set of *Passage to Marseilles*. And, when they began filming *To Have and Have Not*, she was understandably nervous making her first film opposite Warner Brothers' biggest star. To add to her concern, she was 19. Bogart was 45.

She need not have worried. Her first line was 'Anybody got a match?' after which she had to catch a box of matches thrown to her by Bogart. Flustered, she kept on dropping the box, blowing take after take. But Bogart was never put out and treated the whole business as simply one of the inevitable hazards of filming and helped her – without any trace of patronizing her – finally to achieve a perfect take.

Before long, their friendship had progressed and it became obvious to everyone working on *To Have and Have Not* that the couple had fallen in love. That the attraction was clearly mutual was soon evidenced by Bacall's habit of scribbling 'Betty Bogart', Betty B. Bogart' and Betty Bacall Bogart' on scraps of paper. They began to cycle around the lot between takes and lunch together.

Hawks took advantage of the growing love affair to have the script rewritten so that their romance eventually was as obvious in the film itself as it was off-set. And, inevitably, what was happening between the two became common knowledge among local gossips and the Hollywood press corps. Bogart was still married to Mayo – in name, at least – and was quoted as saying that he did not wish to break up the marriage. But he was equally determined not to carry out the affair with Bacall in a clandestine manner and soon there were scarifying fights and scenes when Mayo discovered what was going on.

Bogart, under Bacall's influence, quit his heavy drinking which, at the beginning of *To Have and Have Not*, had resulted in a

Left: Bogart and Bacall with the British economist Sir Norman Angell and director Howard Hawks on the set of *To Have and Have Not*.

run-in with Hawks when he returned to the set suffering from the effect of too many lunch-time martinis. In turn, he initiated Bacall into the pleasures of sailing on his yacht *The Sluggy* (named for Mayo). Before long, Bacall was totally at home on the boat and spent more and more time with Bogart at the Newport Beach Club.

On one occasion club members were scandalized when the two of them appeared on board the yacht one morning, after clearly having spent the night together. Honour was satisfied, however, by the appearance on deck of a married couple – friends of Bogart's – who persuaded everyone that they had been acting as chaperones. On another occasion, however, Mayo turned up on board *The Sluggy*, clearly hoping to catch her husband and Bacall. Bacall hid until Bogart, who was not on the boat at the time, returned and succeeded in getting the irate Mayo to leave.

Later, it was alleged that at a yacht club dinner, Bogart had proposed a toast to : 'My fiancée, Betty Bacall, the future Mrs Bogart.' And, when shooting was completed on *To Have and Have Not*, he spent a weekend on *The Sluggy* with Mayo to tell her that he wanted to finish their marriage. He left her, only to return again to make the first of a series of abortive attempts at a reconciliation.

Bogart had made *Conflict* (1945) before *To Have and Have Not*, playing a wife-murderer in a lacklustre, routine crime melodrama which, however, was given a better

critical and box-office reception than it deserved, as it was released after the huge success of *To Have and Have Not*. The latter film had received a highly encouraging reception at a sneak preview held in Huntington and, on its release, scored heavily with the public.

The film's success effectively killed off any chances of a reconciliation between Bogart and Mayo. The romance between him and Bacall was now no longer simply a subject of gossip but was all too glowingly obvious in their scenes together in the film. Bogart had handed Bacall the movie on a plate and

Above: 'If you want anything, all you have to do is whistle.' The attraction between Bogart and Bacall is clear to all who watch the movie *To Have and Have Not* (Warner Bros.).

Far left: A happy informal picture of Bogart with the woman who was to become the most important in his life, Betty Bacall.

ensured that she became a star with this one picture. And her line: 'If you want anything, all you have to do is whistle', became an instant classic cinema quotation. When one re-views *To Have and Have Not*, however, it becomes obvious that it is a rather slackly handled piece of work which more often than not fails to make the most of its dramatic highlights. But that hardly matters, since the film endures as a monument to one of the legendary Hollywood romances, one that in no small way helped the film to make a fortune for Warner Brothers.

Said *The Sunday Times*: 'On these familiar paths, Bogart moves with his old nonchalant ease, and a pause now and then to take in Miss Bacall: still waters running so deep as to be indistinguishable from stagnation, sulky fire running so hot as to be indistinguishable from a frost. I wouldn't say the film hasn't, in the absence of anything better, its enjoyable moments, but I could use something better.' *Monthly Film Bulletin* found in *To Have and Have Not* that 'neither the plot nor the setting is convincing and Humphrey Bogart has an over-familiar task as the

Early in their romance, Bogart and Bacall had many pleasurable moments aboard his yacht *The Sluggy*, on which he taught her some of the intricacies of sailing.

HUMPHREY BOGART "To HAVE AND HAVE NOT" WARNER BROS.

toughly sentimental Harry. Lauren Bacall shows such real talent and personality as to maintain interest in a not very interesting film.' *Today's Cinema* stated: 'Newcomer Lauren Bacall certainly has an individual personality and invites one's interest in her future work but it is Humphrey Bogart who dominates the portrayal and the artistes.' What no contemporary writer was able to comment upon was the bizarre fact that in the film Bacall's singing voice had been dubbed, improbably but effectively, by Andy Williams.

Bogart was now triumphantly at the top at the studio and, after a brief telephone conversation with Jack L. Warner, he signed a 15-year contract with Warner Brothers, agreeing to make one film for them each year at $200000, along with $1000 a week while he was on location. In all the contract, which also permitted him to make other films outside the studio, was worth over $3000000.

The studio wasted no time in capitalizing on their newly-discovered romantic team and Bogart and Bacall were put straight into *The Big Sleep* (1946), again under Howard

Hawks' direction. The movie was based on Raymond Chandler's detective novel and, despite the claims of screenwriters William Faulkner, Leigh Brackett and Jules Furthman, together with director Hawks and the film's stars, that they could make no sense of the convoluted plot during the making of *The Big Sleep*, the movie emerged as a classic *film noir* and showcased Bogart at his best as private eye Philip Marlowe. The storyline had him hired by a millionaire to rescue his nymphomaniac daughter from a blackmailer and soon finding himself up to his shoulder holster in mystery, mayhem and murder. Bogart's performance was tough, sharp and witty and his scenes with Bacall as the wise-cracking older daughter were even more assured than those they had played in *To Have and Have Not*. For many, *The Big Sleep* is the classic of the Bogart movie canon and certainly his Philip Marlowe is almost as rounded a character as Sam Spade was in *The Maltese Falcon*. The cast was completed by an excellent roster of character actors, including John Ridgely, Martha Vickers, Dorothy Malone and the cinema's eternal fall-

A poster for Warner Brothers' *To Have and Have Not*. Bogart owned a fishing boat and was persuaded to smuggle a wounded French resistance leader out of Martinique.

45

A rural fishing scene from *Conflict* (Warner Bros.), in which Bogart, after murdering his wife, pays court to her younger sister, Alexis Smith.

guy, Elisha Cook Jr, in a typical role.

In *The Big Sleep*, despite the lacunae in the plot and inconsistencies in its exposition, all the elements came together in a way that leaves one not wanting to see the movie changed in any way. Proof of its unique qualities was offered in Michael Winner's gratuitous and quite terrible remake in 1978 in which he moved the locale from Los Angeles to London and audiences from tedium to torpor. Philip Marlowe has been variously portrayed in the cinema; Dick Powell played the character in *Farewell My Lovely* (1946), Robert Montgomery in *Lady in the Lake* (1946), James Garner in 1969's *Marlowe*, Elliott Gould in Robert Altman's appalling *The Long Goodbye* in 1973 and twice by Robert Mitchum, in *Farewell My Lovely* in 1975 and in 1978's *The Big Sleep*. Bogart triumphantly remains the character's archetype.

The critics by and large liked the movie, although they commented on what they felt to be its excessive (for the time) violence. *Kine Weekly* called it: 'A Bogart beanfeast

– or perhaps bloodbath is a more appropriate term', while the *Spectator* said of it that: 'There are murders by bullet and poison, blackmailing and personal violence of a type notorious in German concentration camps. And I have to admit, I enjoyed every minute of it . . .' The *Sunday Express* found it 'a bullet-riddled thriller in the *Laura* class', and *Motion Picture Herald*: 'A highly complicated tale that rivets attention to the screen for almost two tight hours.'

Filming *The Big Sleep* brought Bogart back into almost daily proximity with Bacall once more and accelerated the final break-up of his marriage. By December 1944, while still making the picture, Bogart told Hollywood gossip columnist Louella Parsons that he and Mayo had once more separated, and while there were to be more scenes, more fights, more reconciliations and further separations, the marriage finally ended. On 10 May, 1945, Mayo obtained a divorce in Las Vegas on the by now traditional Hollywood grounds of mental cruelty. Bogart settled a large sum of money on her and gave her

The Big Sleep (Warner Bros.) was a big success for Bogart as Raymond Chandler's private eye Philip Marlowe. A confusing and complicated film, it re-united Bogart and Bacall, and audiences loved their witty dialogue.

ownership of one of the Safeway Stores he owned, and Mayo returned to Portland, Oregon. Six years later she died, reportedly after a long illness brought about by alcoholism.

Eleven days after the divorce, on 21 May, 1945, Bogart and Betty were married by municipal Judge H. H. Shettler at the Ohio home of Bogart's writer friend Louis Bromfield. The ceremony was short and Bogart, who according to Betty, liked to cry at weddings, cried at his own.

He was 45 and Betty was just 20. Confounding all the Hollywood cynics, their's was to be an almost idyllically happy marriage. There were plenty of disagreements – Bogart loved to play chess, Betty hated it, he liked to go to bed early while she enjoyed staying up late – but their sparring was carried out in a spirit of loving banter, with none of the rancour that had characterized his years with Mayo. Bogart had married late for the final time and Betty was clever enough to appreciate that he was set in his ways. She learned to get him to agree to what

she wanted by a method he was not only well aware of but secretly approved, namely that of deliberate misdirection. He was usually perfectly certain that she was carefully manipulating him to come around to what she wanted – and he liked it. He became a happily married man and, later, a contented family man. Bogart had at last found contentment in marriage and turned out to be almost ridiculously uxorious. He no longer found the need to drink heavily now that he was secure in both his personal and professional lives. When he had been agonizing whether or not to marry Betty, his friend Peter Lorre had told him: 'It's better to have five good years than none at all.' Bogart was determined only to have good years – and he did.

He and Betty appeared together briefly for a joke at the end of Two Guys from Milwaukee (1946), a silly comedy starring Dennis Morgan, Jack Carson and Joan Leslie and then went into The Two Mrs Carrolls (1947), an overwrought melodrama based on a stage play which had starred Elizabeth Bergner.

HUMPHREY BOGART · BARBARA STANWYCK · ALEXIS SMITH

Warners'

"The Two Mrs. Carrolls"

Bogart was cast, improbably as it turned out, as a psychopathic painter who killed his first wife and then had a go at his second, played in a hysterical style by Barbara Stanwyck. The British settings were ludicrous and the movie, directed by Peter Godfrey, did nothing for Bogart. Critical reactions, however, were mostly good, with *The Star* commenting that the film was: 'Blazingly good. Bogart with his grim and gloomy charm gives a good suggestion of growing insanity', while *Today's Cinema* said: 'A murder thriller of the very highest order, replete with crackling action . . . with Bogart truly gripping as the demented, tortured killer' and *Kine Weekly*, commenting on its strong feminine appeal and the presence of Bogart, which ensured its commercial success, added that: 'Bogart acts with conviction and considerable dramatic force . . .'

His next film was *Dead Reckoning* (1947), made for Columbia under the direction of John Cromwell, and cast Bogart as a Second World War veteran investigating the murder of an army buddy. The script, by Oliver H.

P. Garrett and Steve Fisher had strong affinities with *The Maltese Falcon* and *The Big Sleep* and its debt to the latter picture was underlined by the performance of co-star Lisabeth Scott. The film emerged as a somewhat typical 1940s *film noir* and, if there was nothing particularly outstanding about the production, Bogart shone, as usual.

The *Sunday Express* commented: 'A characteristic Humphrey Bogart job which is probably commendation enough', while *Today's Cinema* said: 'The dynamic personality of Humphrey Bogart dominates the whole picture, and his playing in the leading role is a fine example of the value of dramatic under-emphasis and intelligent modulations in voice and expression. The basically melodramatic plot has been treated with such skill by the director that its tricks and turns lose their intrinsic implausibility and take on an air of absorbing realism.' But there were comments that indicated that Bogart, in critical eyes, at least, was beginning to be typecast as sardonic, wisecracking detectives and quasi private eyes. Said *Tribune*: 'Holly-

Above: A showcard for *The Two Mrs Carrolls* (Warner Bros.). In one of his poorer films, Bogart was a psychopath who killed his first wife and attempted the same with the second, Barbara Stanwyck, who has the drop on him in this scene.

Far left: Not quite the usual image of Bogart. He and Betty hold a model bride and groom after their marriage. Note also the horseshoe on the door.

Bogart made *Dead Reckoning* for Columbia, and was co-starred with Lizabeth Scott in a story in which he played a paratrooper seeking out the murderer of a friend.

HUMPHREY
BOGART

LIZABETH
SCOTT

JOHN CROMWELL'S DEAD RECKONING

with

MORRIS   CHARLES   WILLIAM   MARVIN   WALLACE
CARNOVSKY   CANE   PRINCE   MILLER   FORD

Screenplay by OLIVER H. P. GARRETT, STEVE FISHER

Directed by JOHN CROMWELL · Produced by SIDNEY BIDDELL

A COLUMBIA PICTUR

wood quite clearly does not know any longer what to do with Bogart. A war story in the manner of *Casablanca* was all right in its day, and a Raymond Chandler thriller about high-minded depravity on the Pacific coast is always pleasurable, but there can be no more *Casablancas*, no more villainous Vichyite policemen while even Chandler's invention must sometimes take a rest.'

Bogart's final film for 1947 reunited him with Bacall under Delmer Daves' direction in *Dark Passage*. It was their third film together. The melodramatic story had Bogart incarcerated in San Quentin for the murder of his wife and breaking out, undergoing plastic surgery and turning detective to prove his innocence of the crime and pinning it on the rightful perpetrator Agnes Moorehead. Bacall played a wealthy artist who believed in his innocence and helped him. Their scenes together gave the movie its real charm and, if it was not a major entry in Bogart's canon, it was, with all its contrivances and limitations, a very enjoyable one.

Critical comment included, from *Today's Cinema*: 'The already compelling development is emphasised by the tense portraiture of Humphrey Bogart . . . presenting another of those studies in baleful concentration. Though fanciful as to its coincidental twists at times, this crime melodrama is an expertly tailored specimen of its own violent type, and its blend of action, suspense, thrill and dynamic characterization effortlessly registers as first rate entertainment for the devotees of the species.' *Kine Weekly* thought it: 'Vintage Bogart', and the *Daily Mail* noted: 'Mr Bogart is a lover who snarls like a blast furnace, and his woeful ballad mostly takes the form of grunts from public call-boxes. While Miss Bacall responds with the monosyllabic mating call that is her special contribution to the art of acting.'

Their happy on-screen relationship in *Dark Passage* was reflected in their off-screen life. Bogart, happily settled into married bliss with Bacall, was now contemplating late fatherhood, after never having wanted children during his first three marriages. During the filming of *Dark Passage*, he had started to take hormone pills to increase his fertility. Unfortunately, side-effects caused his hair to fall out although it eventually grew back again. He was forced, and he hated it, to wear a toupee for the rest of his screen career.

For the first 16 years of their marriage, Bogart and Betty lived in an apartment on Sunset Strip and then bought a house in Benedict Canyon which had belonged to Hedy Lamarr, complete with a butler named Fred. While there was still affectionate banter between the two on subjects on which they held opposing views, Bogart and Betty were united in their political leanings, being basically liberals who supported the Democrats. Bogart had been strong in his espousal of Roosevelt and he and Betty had helped in the election of Harry S. Truman.

In 1947, however, the United States was feverishly in the grip of anti-Communist hysteria with Red-baiting demagogue Senator Joe McCarthy making a name for himself and stirring up hostility towards anyone with Communist connections – tenuous or otherwise. No doubt motivated by the obvious media publicity it would bring to the accusers, the House Committee on Un-American Activities decided that Hollywood was the perfect target for their investigations. And, of course, they uncovered the hoped-for evidence of Communist cells operating in the movie capital.

The so-called 'Unfriendly Ten' – Alvah Bessie, Herbert Biberman, Lester Cole, Edward Dmytryk, Ring Lardner Jr, John Howard Lawson (who had written the screenplay for Bogart's 1943 movie *Action in the North Atlantic*), Albert Maltz, Sam Ornitz, Adrian Scott and Dalton Trumbo –

Bogart and his wife were among a group of Hollywood stars who flew to Washington in 1947 to protest about the way the House Committee on Un-American Activities was conducting its business. From left to right in the front row are Geraldine Brooks, June Havoc, Marsha Hunt, Lauren Bacall, Richard Conte and Evelyn Keyes. Behind them are Paul Henreid, Bogart (the spokesman), Gene Kelly and Danny Kaye.

were called to Washington to testify before the HUAC. It was an event which shocked Hollywood, and John Huston organized a planeload of movie celebrities to fly to Washington and lobby on behalf of the Unfriendly Ten.

The gesture backfired, however, when the Ten took the stand and refused to testify that they were innocent, instead falling back on the First Amendment. Bogart, who had, like the rest, been assured that the Ten were being maligned unjustly, admitted his mistake. The admission, like his espousal of their cause, was a typically brave course of action since, with the country in the grip of anti-Communist frenzy, it was a decidedly dangerous thing even to admit support of accused Reds. Bogart told a *Newsweek* reporter: 'We went in there green and they beat our brains out. But in the shuffle we became adopted by the Communists, and I ended up with my picture on the front page of *The Daily Worker*. I detest Communism just as any decent American does. My name will not be found on any Communist front organization nor as a sponsor of anything Communistic. That the trip was ill advised, even foolish, I am ready to admit. I am an American and very likely, like a good many of the rest of you, sometimes a foolish and impetuous American.'

The Unfriendly Ten all served prison sentences. Cynics might be excused for thinking that, while the HUAC wanted the publicity that accompanied the indictment of Hollywood personalities, they were too shrewd to pick on major talents in the movie colony and so help to wreck the film industry. This admittedly uncharitable view is endorsed by director Billy Wilder, who was quoted as saying of the Unfriendly Ten that: 'Two of them had talent – and the other eight were just unfriendly.'

After briefly appearing, unbilled, along with Jack Carson, Errol Flynn, Dennis Morgan, Janis Paige, Eleanor Parker and Alexis Smith in a film-within-a-film in 1948's *Always Together*, parodying *Stella Dallas* and causing *Time* to say: 'Best thing in the show: Humphrey Bogart', Bogart made another film which remains one of his classic performances and one of which he was justly proud.

Director John Huston called Bogart and asked him to appear in *The Treasure of the Sierra Madre*, a film he had been wanting to make for years and for which he had just received the go-ahead from Warner Brothers.

Bogart was smart enough to realize that the character he was to play, the tough American prospector Fred C. Dobbs, involved with two other Americans in a hunt

On the set of *The Treasure of the Sierra Madre* (Warner Bros.), one of the screen's classics and a triumph for Bogart. Bogart, Walter Huston and Tim Holt relax with some iced drinks during a break in the strenuous filming.

Bogart, Walter Huston and Tim Holt as three gold prospectors in *The Treasure of the Sierra Madre* (Warner Bros.). Walter Huston won an Oscar as best supporting actor for his performance, and his son John Huston the Oscar for best direction.

for gold in Mexico, was an excellent one but not the best in the movie. That went to Huston's father Walter as the oldest of the would-be prospectors and he won a well-deserved Oscar as best supporting actor for his performance, while John Huston picked up Academy Awards for both his direction and his screenplay, based on the pseudonymous novel by the mysterious B. Traven.

The Treasure of the Sierra Madre was filmed on location in Mexico and was one of the first major postwar movies to be made entirely outside a studio. Huston's obsessive quest for reality in the film's backgrounds made filming an arduous and often hazardous process. If a site for filming looked too easy to reach, Huston selected another that was more difficult to get to, and among the natural hazards encountered by the actors and crew were insects, terrible weather alternating between tropical downpours and burning sun and bad food, with Betty – who accompanied Bogart on location – often turning cook to provide her husband with ham and eggs.

The movie was a gripping and deeply etched study of man's greed, and in it every performance is memorable. Even taking Walter Huston's Oscar into account, Bogart's Fred C. Dobbs, slowly and believably changing from an unmotivated drifter to a cold-blooded killer, is one of his greatest performances. He finally died at the hand of a Mexican bandit, despite Jack L. Warner's agonized opposition to the death of his biggest star on-screen, a far cry from the 1930s when Bogart's screen appearances almost always presaged his violent death in the last reel. In the movie, Bogart is not simply a superb screen star but a memorable and immensely powerful actor. *The Treasure of the Sierra Madre* was one of the studio's more expensive – $3000000 – to date and, surprisingly, disappointed at the box office. But, for all Bogart aficionados, it remains a classic, one of his films that can be seen and re-seen with enjoyment.

Monthly Film Bulletin claimed the film as: 'This powerful story of life in the raw, superbly acted by Humphrey Bogart', while the *Sunday Graphic* said: 'The success of the film depends on Bogart, his face concealed for most of the film behind a façade of whiskers and grime. He plays it perfectly', and the *Daily Graphic* stated that it was: 'A film that will raise Hollywood's prestige to Himalayan heights . . . an immense, dramatic, ironic masculine film.' For the *News Chronicle* it was: 'A sweeping canvas of banditry and gold-digging . . . depicted with wit, irony, insight and verve.'

For Bogart, it was simply a triumph.

THE RAT PACK AND THE AFRICAN QUEEN

Bogart's last picture for 1948 saw him working again with John Huston in *Key Largo*, adapted by Huston and Richard Brooks from a stage play by Maxwell Anderson and its stage origins were carried over into the movie. The action took place almost entirely inside a Florida hotel where deported gangster Edward G. Robinson held its occupants – including Bogart and Bacall – hostage. The movie was a talk piece rather than an action one, although there was a stunning climax and, yet again, Bogart's sheer professionalism, allied to his charisma, carried it through. Claire Trevor's performance as a blowsy singer won her an Oscar as best supporting actress and the movie won more fans for Bogart and more box-office profits for

Warner Brothers. Part of the success of the movie was undoubtedly due to its strong echoes of *The Petrified Forest*, with Robinson in a reworking of the Duke Mantee role.

In 1949 Bogart, with Robert Lord and Mark Hellinger, formed his own production company Santana Productions, named after his boat, and his first movie for Santana, made for Columbia, cast him as a tough lawyer defending juvenile murderer John Derek (making his film debut). Nicholas Ray's direction was adequate but he did nothing to justify his current cult status and only Bogart really emerged with any credit from what was a minor movie, *Knock on any Door*. Said *The Film*: 'A great big bore. It is not so much a film as a tract', but *The Times* noted

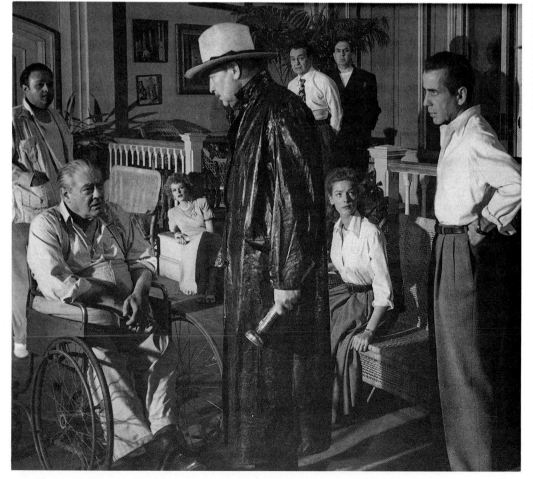

In *Key Largo* (Warner Bros.), Bogart was trapped in a Florida hotel by Edward G. Robinson and his gang. From the left: Dan Seymour, Lionel Barrymore, Claire Trevor, Marc Lawrence, Edward G. Robinson, Thomas Gomez, Lauren Bacall and Bogart.

that: 'Mr Bogart stirs himself out of his impassivity to make the barrister's pleading earnest and eloquent.'

His second 1949 film, *Tokyo Joe*, also made for Santana and Columbia, was simply terrible. In it, Bogart played an American in post-war Japan caught up in blackmail and smuggling to save his daughter, with tepid direction by Stuart Heisler. The *Daily Mail* noted: 'The setting of occupied Japan may be new, but nothing else that takes place in it is.' The *News of the World* said: 'With anybody but Humphrey Bogart starring in this wildly fabulous drama of occupied Japan, it would have deserved and received an all-round thumbs down . . . It must be the tremendous sincerity and authority at his command that makes palatable such films as *Tokyo Joe*.' Clearly, for all the usual star rantings against the terrible stories picked for them by their studios, Bogart, like so many other movie actors, was far from infallible when it came to picking subjects in which to star for his own company.

If 1949 marked a hiatus in Bogart's film career, it also marked a new development in his private life. On 6 January 1949, his son Stephen was born. Bogart was 49 and clearly the hormone pills he had been taking had proved a resounding success. Given his character, it might well have been assumed that fatherhood was the last thing Bogart wanted. In reality, however, Bogart was a good and proud father even if, as he once confided to a reporter: 'I don't understand my children and I think they don't understand me, and all I can say is thank God for Betty.'

Betty had decided, while she was carrying Steve, that the Bogarts should move from their Benedict Canyon home to another, and bigger, home. As usual, she had to work on her husband to get him to agree to the change and finally, despite his objections to living among the 'rich creeps' of the Hollywood elite, they bought a house in exclusive Holmby Hills. And it was here that one of the most enduring – and likable – Hollywood legends found its home.

Despite his claimed dislike of Hollywood society, Bogart was now firmly part of the movie capital's royalty. He and Betty would go to phoney Prince Mike Romanoff's elite Beverly Hills restaurant for lunch arriving at 12.30 sharp and taking up their regular place in the second booth on the left. There, able to see everything and everyone, they would hold court with their friends and drinking and talking companions, most notably Frank Sinatra, John Huston, Judy Garland and her husband Sid Luft, James Van Heusen the songwriter, writer Nathanial Benchley, literary agent Irving 'Swifty' Lazar, Romanoff himself and the David Nivens.

Above: Bogart and Bacall show off their new son, Stephen Humphrey, soon after his birth in 1949.

Writer Joe Hyams carried the news of the formation of the Holmby Hills Rat Pack (so called, according to myth, after Betty's comment on seeing the regular gathering: 'I see the rat pack is all here'), in his column in the New York *Herald Tribune*.

He wrote: 'The Holmby Hills Rat Pack held its first annual meeting last night at Romanoff's restaurant in Beverly Hills and elected officers for the coming year. Named to executive positions were: Frank Sinatra, pack master; Judy Garland, first vice president; Lauren Bacall, den mother; Sid Luft, cage master; Humphrey Bogart, rat in charge of public relations; Irving Lazar, recording secretary and treasurer; Nathanial Benchley, historian.

'The only members of the organization not voted into office are David Niven, Michael Romanoff and James Van Heusen. Mr Niven, an Englishman, Mr Romanoff, a Russian, and Mr Van Heusen, an American, protested that they were discriminated against because of their national origins. Mr Sinatra, who was acting chairman of the

Far left: Off the set of *Key Largo* Bogart chats with the director John Huston, who had already been associated with some of his best films – *High Sierra, The Maltese Falcon, The Treasure of the Sierra Madre* – and was later to direct Bogart in *The African Queen*.

meeting, refused to enter their protests . . .

'Mr Bogart, who was spokesman, said the organization has no specific function other than "the relief of boredom and the perpetuation of independence. We admire ourselves and don't care for anyone else . . . membership is open to free-minded individuals who don't care what anyone thinks about them".'

Bogart's statement admirably encapsulates his own attitude to life, one that he always lived by. The Rat Pack continued its informal meetings at Romanoffs and Bogart's home until his death. After his death, Sinatra took over the basic idea to form the notorious Clan, with such members as Sammy Davis Jr, Joey Bishop, Shirley Maclaine and Peter Lawford, but it never really achieved the cameraderie and sheer *joi de vivre* of the original. Bogart was the motive force behind the Rat Pack and, like everything he did, it was inimitable.

Chain Lightning (1950), again directed by Stuart Heisler, took him back to Warner Brothers as a one-time bomber pilot engaged in testing new jet aircraft. It was a routine affair and nothing to write home about, although *The Observer* called it: '. . . one of those technically perfect pictures that Hollywood turns out almost automatically.' *Time*, however, stated that it was: 'A great rush of supersonic hot air . . . with Humphrey Bogart as the devil-may-care test pilot, its heroics are built to scale. Tough guy Bogart still conveys emotion by baring his teeth in a grimace that gentlefolks reserve for the moment after biting into a wormy apple.'

In a Lonely Place (1950), again made for Santana and Columbia with Nicholas Ray of *Knock on any Door* directing again, was his best for his own production company, a moody *film noir* that tends to be badly underrated, although it is a firm favourite among fans of the star. In the film Bogart, shedding his tough-guy image with considerable success, was a Hollywood screenwriter accused of murder and involved with Gloria Grahame. The movie succeeds better than most of the genre in giving an acid and probably accurate picture of the less glamorous aspects of film making and the film capital. His superb performance, along with an excellent one by Grahame and first-class playing by the minor performers – including Carl Benton Reid and Bogart's old friend from his theatre days, Robert Warwick – was noted by the *Motion Picture Herald* which wrote: 'He catches admirably the emotional ups and downs of a deeply disturbed individual, grasping at straws for a return to normalcy', and the *New Statesman* commented that: 'Bogart gives his best performance for many a year.' Bogart made the film, thereby knocking another nail into the coffin of the auteur theory which tends to hold that *In a Lonely Place* is a Nicholas Ray picture rather than a Bogart one.

Bogart's final film for Warner Brothers was 1951's *The Enforcer*, known in Britain as *Murder, Inc.* Pacy direction by Bretaigne Windust, a taut Martin Rackin script and a stand-out performance by Bogart as a crusading District Attorney determined to eradicate a professional murder organization combined to make the movie a memorable one, and a return to the studio's habit of creating films out of current headlines. British critics reacted against its toughness and violence, with the *Evening News* saying: 'Enough horror for the strongest stomach. Not for a moment is its intention of being ugly softened by comedy or love-making', a sentiment echoed by the *Daily Mirror*: 'A bloodbath for the boys.' For *The Star*, it was written that: 'At 51, Bogart has attained that agelessness that time bestows on all the best personality actors; and his trademarks – the lazy sewage snarl, the gnarled lisp of a voice, the face that looks like a triumph of plastic surgery – should see him safely through another ten years at the top.' Sadly, that was

Bogart with director Nicholas Ray considering a scene for *In a Lonely Place*, which was made by Bogart's new independent production company, Santana, with Columbia.

In *The Enforcer*, Bogart's last film for Warner Brothers, he and his colleagues drag a swamp used by Murder Inc. as a dump for their victims, and then have the task of identifying the countless shoes they discover.

not to be, although his greatest triumph was only a year away.

After *The Enforcer*, it was back again to Santana and Columbia for *Sirocco* (1951), a pedestrian effort directed by Curtis Bern- hardt that merits attention simply because Bogart, seemingly effortlessly, turns in a per- formance that lifts the movie out of the me- diocre rut in which it really deserves to stay. The inspiration may have been *Casablanca*, with Bogart as a gun-runner in 1925 Damas- cus, but the realization was strictly run-of- the-mill. The *Monthly Film Bulletin* reviewer wrote that: 'The story follows a pattern fam- iliar since *Casablanca*. The plot development is slow and lacks conviction, as does the Da- mascus atmosphere. Bogart himself, walking about the catacombs in a raincoat, gives a performance so emotionless and expression- less as to suggest a parody of his own acting technique.' *Kine Weekly* was more generous, writing of Bogart's impressive performance.

In 1950, John Huston had telephoned Bo- gart and told him: 'Hey, old son I've got a great property. The hero's a lowlife and since you're the biggest lowlife in town the part is ideal for you.' It was not, however, until 1951 that Bogart began filming his finest pic- ture, *The African Queen*, in what was then still the Belgian Congo.

The intervening time was taken up by Huston persuading producer Sam Spiegel and his backers that it would not be absolute madness to shoot a Technicolor movie in the middle of Africa, involving the enormous expense of sending the precious negative back to Britain for processing, to say nothing of the other logistical and budgetary prob- lems that would inevitably be encountered on such an inaccessible location. As usual Huston, who enjoyed uncomfortable loca- tions much more than most of his actors, prevailed and, after several re-writes of the script, arrived in London to bring his stars – Bogart and Katharine Hepburn – to Africa.

He discovered that Spiegel's backers had decided not to participate in *The African Queen* and had to persuade Bogart and Hep- burn to accept deferment against future profits for part of their salaries. Bogart took $35000 against 25 per cent of profits and Hepburn $65000 against 10 per cent of the profits, Bogart deferring $125000 of his fee, and Hepburn $65000. That settled, they flew

to Rome on their way to Ponthierville, the headquarters of the film, and the river Ruiki on which most of the movie's action was to be shot. Betty accompanied her husband on location and soon, like the rest of the cast and crew, found it to be an ordeal so horrendous as to make the rigours experienced making *The Treasure of the Sierra Madre* seem, in retrospect, like no more than a pleasant vacation.

The Congo – as this writer knows to his cost – is no romantic rain forest but an unpleasant combination of insects, snakes, wild animals and tropical illnesses. Soon everyone in the company – with the exception of Bogart and Betty who never drank the water, Bogart even taking to brushing his teeth in whisky – were suffering from dysentery. Bogart hated the place. His co-star, however, took to Africa with her usual efficiency, claiming on one occasion that it was 'utterly divine'. Her cheerful acceptance of the horrors of mosquitoes, leeches, high humidity and general low spirits on the part of most of the members of *The African Queen* company finally drove her co-star to declare: 'Damn Hepburn! Damn her, she's so goddam cheerful. She's got ants in her pants, mildew in her shoes, and she's still cheerful.

I build a solid wall of whisky between me and the bugs. She doesn't drink, and she breezes through it all as though it were a weekend in Connecticut!' Later he was to tell reporters, after completing the film: 'She won't let anybody get a word in edgewise and she keeps repeating what a superior person she is. Later, you get a load of the babe stalking through the African jungle as though she had beaten Livingstone to it. Her shirttail is carefully torn for casual effect and is flapping out of her jeans. She pounces on the flora and fauna with a home movie camera like a kid going to his first Christmas tree, and she blunders within ten feet of a wild boar's tusks for a closeup of the beast. About every other minute she wrings her hands in ecstacy and says, "What divine natives! What divine morning-glories!" Brother, your brow goes up . . . is this something from *The Philadelphia Story*?'

In fact, Bogart's outbursts were simply part of the tough-guy public persona, the hard-cased existentialist he liked to present to the uninformed. He and Hepburn got on splendidly together and their screen partnership in *The African Queen* remains one of the truly great partnerships in the cinema's history.

Above: Bogart and Hepburn sparked off great performances from each other in *The African Queen* (United Artists), for which Bogart won an Oscar as Best Actor.

Far left: Charlie Allnutt, the hard-bitten tugboat skipper, played by Humphrey Bogart, relaxes on his boat with Katharine Hepburn, who played the prim, starchy missionary who shares a hazardous voyage with him in *The African Queen* (United Artists).

Bogart and Hepburn being prepared for a colour screen test while shooting parts of *The African Queen* (United Artists) at Isleworth Studios. The gentle English countryside was a change from the insects, leeches and snakes of the Congo.

The African Queen (1951) was based on a 1935 novel by C. S. Forester and cast Bogart as a hard-drinking, tough Canadian, Charlie Allnutt, who is conned by Katharine Hepburn's equally tough, if prim, missionary into taking his battered tug-boat down an uncharted African river in East Africa during the First World War to attack and destroy a German gunboat. Allnutt had originally been a Cockney but the role had been changed to allow for Bogart's accent.

Bogart and Hepburn dominated *The African Queen*, which was virtually a two-hander, appearing together on screen for about 90 per cent of the picture. Their performances were a masterpiece of ensemble acting

and a triumphant *tour de force*. Natural humour leavened the tension and the drama and it was a rare pleasure to watch Bogart's dissipated Allnutt slowly showing his soft centre under Hepburn's constant browbeating while she, in turn, unbent so that their growing romantic attachment became not simply dramatically valid but also the true climax of the movie, more so than the final destruction of the German gunboat on Lake Victoria moments after the couple had been married by the ship's Captain in deference to their last wishes.

Bogart afficionados will always argue about which of his films is the best. There may be many contenders but, for its sheer vitality, pervading spirit of human companionship and joy and for its ability to provide complete enjoyment, time after time, *The African Queen* deserves the ultimate accolade.

Bogart's Hollywood peers could hardly fail to take notice of his superb portrayal and they duly nominated him for an Academy Award as best actor. Hepburn received an Oscar nomination as best actress and Huston one for best director. All were deserved but, in 1951, only Bogart stepped on the stage at Hollywood's Pantages Theatre to receive his long overdue Academy Award, beating, rightly, nominees Marlon Brando for *A Streetcar Named Desire*, Montgomery Clift for *A Place in the Sun*, Arthur Kennedy for *Bright Victory* and Fredric March for *Death of a Salesman*. It was a moment to be savoured and a fitting climax – though not an end – to a remarkable screen career.

Typically, Bogart did not allow his Oscar to change his attitude to movie making. Reportedly, his young son Steve took the statuette the next morning and threw it at his father and Bogart himself saw it for what it was, telling a columnist: 'The way to survive an Oscar is never to try to win another one. You've seen what happens to some Oscar winners. They spend the rest of their lives turning down scripts while searching for the great role to win another one. Hell, I hope

I'm never even nominated again. It's meat-and-potato roles for me from now on.'

In fact, one of those 'meat-and-potato' roles, that of the demented Captain Queeg in 1954's *The Caine Mutiny*, won him another nomination.

Of *The African Queen*, *Today's Cinema* said: 'Bogart is entirely credible. It is a performance of rare comic distinction', and the *Daily Telegraph* added : 'Bogart's Allnutt is something quite new. He has chosen to play so many solemn neurotics that you might not suppose him capable of such kindly, likable humanity', while the *Sunday Times* commented: 'As for Bogart, he has shaken himself out of the routine performance he has been giving lately and gone back to the actor he was years ago.' In the *New Yorker*, John McCarten wrote: 'Hepburn and Bogart come up with a couple of remarkable performances, and it's fortunate that they do, for the movie concentrates on them so single-mindedly that any conspicuous uncertainty in their acting would have left the whole thing high and dry.'

If there were to be no more great movies like *The African Queen* Bogart's remaining ten films, and even the least worthy of them, were to show the actor in full command of his material, amply demonstrating real star quality of a kind rare in the cinema and uniquely his own.

Perhaps his best part – Bogart as the hard-swearing, hard-drinking skipper with the soft centre chugging up the Congo in his boat *The African Queen* (United Artists).

THE LAST FEW REELS

Bogart and Betty continued their secure and happy married life, entertaining their fellow members of the Holmby Hills Rat Pack at the house. By now, despite his half-hearted protestations, Bogart was the complete family man, proud that his son Steve was taking after him in his independence and self-confident spirit and, in the family tradition, finding nicknames for other people which included 'Blubber Head' and 'Mr Do in the Pants'. And, on 23 August 1952, his daughter – named Leslie Howard after his good friend and sometime co-star – was born, completing the family. The tough outer shell that Bogart had so long presented to the outer world had long ago vanished, revealing the warm, human and even sentimental real man beneath.

He returned to Twentieth Century-Fox for the first time since his unhappy days at the studio in the 1930s to make *Deadline – U.S.A.* (1952), a tense and well made drama that cast him as a crusading newspaper editor who ignored threats and intimidation to expose a powerful crime boss. Writer-director Richard Brooks (who had been the co-writer of *Key Largo*) kept the proceedings brisk and tense, even if, in the final analysis, there was too much high-minded talk padding out the melodramatic happenings. 'Humphrey Bogart', said *Today's Cinema*, 'gives a characteristically tense and interesting performance as the editor, and makes his lines hit home . . .' and *Kine Weekly* averred that Bogart was: 'Ideal casting in the leading role . . .'

His next, *Battle Circus* (1953), for MGM, was a stinker. The movie, a tepid and unconvincing affair about the romance between Bogart's army doctor and June Allyson as a nurse in a Korean mobile army hospital (shades of *M*A*S*H*, but unfortunately without the conscious humour of the film and the television series), was written and directed by Richard Brooks and while, visually, he achieved some moments of effective power, the basic script and dialogue were strictly from soap opera. The *News Chronicle* was scathing, saying: 'The invasion of Korea by MGM, Humphrey Bogart and June Allyson . . . is one of the most unsavoury battles fought on celluloid. It contemptuously treats the suffering of the soldier as mere props to the wooing of Lieut June Allyson by Major Humphrey Bogart', while the *Sunday Chronicle* added: '*Battle Circus* ruins an effective and sincere semi-documentary tribute to the US Medical Service in Korea by casting a galaxy of showgirls as nurses and cooking up a glutinous box-office love affair between Bogart and June Allyson . . . and if war must be made into

The Bogarts' two children, Stephen and daughter Leslie Howard. Born in 1952, Leslie was named after the actor and friend who helped Bogart get an important break in *The Petrified Forest*.

An intimate picture of Humphrey Bogart and Betty Bacall which conveys the affection they felt for each other from their first meeting until the end of his life.

a circus, then we must expect circus girls, however thinly disguised they may be as Army nurses.'

Beat the Devil (1954), made as a co-production between Santana and Romulus, reunited Bogart with John Huston and emerged as very much a curate's egg as it spoofed, among others, *The Maltese Falcon* and *Across the Pacific*, and while the cast had a good time filming it, the movie failed to attract general audiences, although it has since become a cult Bogart favourite. Bogart himself was later to be quoted as saying: 'Only the phonies think it's funny. It's a mess.'

Bogart himself had bought James Helvick's novel, knowing that Huston could not afford it, and the director had two writers

– Peter Viertel and Anthony Veiller – come up with separate screenplays which he then rewrote himself, sending the draft to Bogart who, when asked by Huston on the telephone if he had read it, replied: 'Couldn't finish it. It was awful.' Back came Huston's cheerful rejoinder: 'Neither could I. Stinker, isn't it?'

Despite this inauspicious start, Bogart shelled out $600000 of his own money and Huston continued to prepare *Beat the Devil* which was to be filmed in Italy. David O. Selznick agreed to the casting of his wife Jennifer Jones as Bogart's romantic interest (although, in the movie, a bemused Gina Lollobrigida is Bogart's screen spouse) but, when the craze for 3–D pictures suddenly hit Hollywood, Selznick panicked, cabling:

'ABANDON PROJECT. TAKE ONE OF MINE. YOU WILL RUIN YOUR CAREER AND JENNIFER'S'. No notice was taken of his agonized plea and the movie, originally conceived as a straight melodrama, was given an uncomfortable tongue-in-cheek treatment by Truman Capote, who was hired because he happened to be living in Rome at the time. He was forced to write against a near-impossible deadline and the finished film shows it all too well, as well as Huston's inability to decide just what kind of film he was making.

The plot of *Beat the Devil* was a complex improbable farrago involving the machinations of a strange crowd of villains and near-villains to get hold of the mining rights to uranium-bearing land on the East African coast and, in the melee of crossing, double and triple crossing that ensued, what pleasure there was to be derived from the film came from the in-jokes that no doubt appealed to the film's makers, but were interesting only to cognoscenti among the relatively sparse audiences who saw the picture.

Bogart played Billy Dannreuther, heading an international melange of crooks – Britain's Robert Morley and Ivor Barnard, Italy's Marco Tulli and Peter Lorre, impersonating a German from Chile named O'Hara and reacting bitterly against its constant mispronunciation in the film as 'O'Horror'. Rounding off the cast were Lollobrigida as Bogart's wife, Jennifer Jones as the flirtatious wife of pukka British sahib Edward Underdown and a bewildered-looking Bernard Lee as a police inspector, who gloried in the screen name of Jack Clayton, the film's producer.

It was this kind of inside gag, carried to extremes throughout the film, that put paid to the chances of *Beat the Devil* at the box-office. There's no doubt that true Bogart fans can find a great deal to like in the picture and, of course, the 'phonies' Bogart spoke about are able to have a field day with the references to past movies and characters. In the end, however, despite all the fun everyone apparently had in Italy making the film, it shows all too strongly Capote's desperate improvisations, and lacks a coherence and point of view to carry it through.

Audiences failed to beat a path into the cinemas showing *Beat the Devil* although the critics were kinder. The *New Statesman* commented that it was: 'A slight, amusing comedy thriller. We shall be disappointed if with John Huston's name attached, we expect more . . .' *Time* thought it to be: 'As elaborate a shaggy dog story as has ever been told.' *The Star* complained: 'Morley is brilliantly Morley, Lorre is lethargically Lorre and Bogart, who had a hand in the production, is brashly Bogart. Clearly, he and Hus-

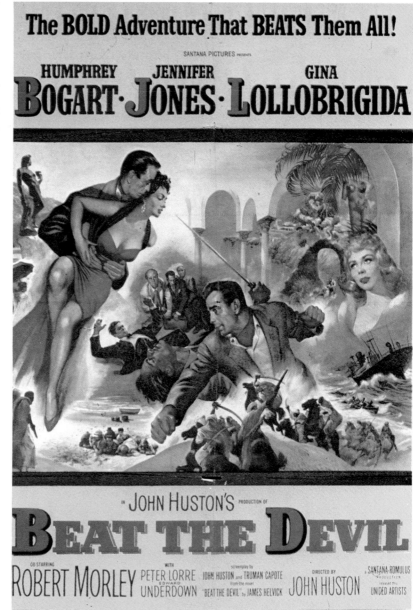

The BOLD Adventure That BEATS Them All!

SANTANA PICTURES PRESENTS

HUMPHREY **BOGART** · JENNIFER **JONES** · GINA **LOLLOBRIGIDA**

IN JOHN HUSTON'S PRODUCTION OF

BEAT THE DEVIL

CO STARRING **ROBERT MORLEY** WITH PETER LORRE EDWARD UNDERDOWN screenplay by JOHN HUSTON and TRUMAN CAPOTE from the novel 'BEAT THE DEVIL' by JAMES HELVICK DIRECTED BY JOHN HUSTON a SANTANA-ROMULUS PRODUCTION released thru UNITED ARTISTS

ton have enjoyed themselves on this film . . . but *Beat the Devil* is hardly the sort of film you expect from men of their achievements. There is an empty ring behind its laughter', and *Sight and Sound*, presumably deciding to abandon for the moment their belief in Huston as auteur, wrote: 'The acting is at times inexpert and at times grossly unsubtle . . . *Beat the Devil* has the air of an expensive house-party joke, a charade which enormously entertained its participants at the time of playing, but which is too private and insufficiently brilliant to justify public performance. The script has some good lines, but meanders hopelessly and badly lacks a climax.'

If *Beat the Devil* were a failure – if an enterprising one – Bogart's next film would win him another Oscar nomination for his performance as the neurotic Captain Queeg

Above: A poster for *Beat the Devil* (United Artists), for which Bogart was co-producer and which was his last film with John Huston. It was an indulgent movie which brought more enjoyment to its principals than to audiences.

Far left: An explosive background for a scene from *Deadline – U.S.A.* (Twentieth Century-Fox), in which Bogart was a crusading newspaper editor fighting to save his paper and expose a crime syndicate.

in the film version of Herman Wouk's best-seller *The Caine Mutiny*. And the fact that the film's director was Edward Dmytryk, who had been one of the Unfriendly Ten for whom Bogart had made his ill-fated trip to Washington in 1947, didn't worry him in the least. Bogart turned out to be the perfect Queeg – indeed, even after seeing Lloyd Nolan on the stage in a theatre dramatization of the court martial scene, it is still impossible to visualize anyone but Bogart in the role – and his powerful central performance, which impressively brought out both the character's brutally psychotic nature and his humanity in final defeat, is memorable and infinitely watchable. His Academy Award nomination was eminently well-deserved. At the Awards ceremony, Bogart was up against Marlon Brando for *On the Waterfront*, Bing Crosby for *The Country Girl*, James Mason for *A Star Is Born* and Dan O'Herlihy for *The Adventures of Robinson Crusoe*. Bogart had beaten Brando when the latter had been nominated for *A Streetcar Named Desire* and Bogart had won for *The African Queen*. Now the roles were reversed and it was Brando who took the Oscar for a strong performance in *On the Waterfront*.

Bogart did not enjoy his next picture *Sabrina* (1954), particularly as it followed the excellent notices he had received for *The Caine Mutiny*. *The Spectator* had said: 'Bogart takes this by no means easy part and wrings every drop of sourness and sadness from it, proving once again that when given the opportunity he is a master at his craft', and for the *News of the World* his performance was 'a memorable and majestic achievement'. *Time* thought that: 'Bogart adds a quality of almost noble despair to the Captain's sufferings' and *Time and Tide* commented: 'Bogart's flickering and writhing . . . surpasses anything he has previously done.'

So his experience making *Sabrina* (1954), known as *Sabrina Fair* in Britain, must have been doubly uncomfortable. He had been pleased to be asked to appear in the movie by Billy Wilder when the originally-cast Cary Grant had dropped out, but he was soon clashing on set with the director and was at his most difficult during the making of the picture. He also clashed with co-star William Holden who was quoted as saying, when Bogart was mentioned subsequently, that 'I'll kill that son of a bitch!' And, although he was not in the habit of saying

Bogart was brilliant as the paranoid Captain Queeg in *The Caine Mutiny* (Columbia), and was nominated for another Oscar. In this scene he battles with a storm, helped by Van Johnson and Robert Francis.

As a romantic lead opposite Audrey Hepburn in *Sabrina* (*Sabrina Fair* in Great Britain) (Paramount) Bogart was not at ease in a role originally intended for Cary Grant.

it, Bogart was reputed to be considerably less than enamoured of his leading lady Audrey Hepburn's acting abilities.

Sabrina itself was a smart reworking of the Cinderella story, based by writer-director Billy Wilder on a play by Samuel Taylor. Bogart played the stuffy elder brother who determines to prevent his playboy brother Holden from marrying chauffeur's daughter Hepburn and, as might be expected in a Hollywood fairy-tale, ends up with the girl himself in the final reel. There may have been ructions on set but the finished product is a slick and witty comedy of manners and, while Bogart was really too old for the romantic role, he gave a first-rate performance whose wryness offsets some of Audrey Hepburn's often cloying gamine charm.

'Only Humphrey Bogart rescues the picture from complete failure . . .' wrote the *Daily Sketch*, and *Today's Cinema* called him: '. . . surprisingly effective in a part which is principally the lightest of comedy'. The *New Yorker* stated that he had turned in a really first-class performance but added: 'There are, alas, quite a few lethargic stretches between the hugs and chuckles.'

Bogart travelled to Rome to make *The Barefoot Contessa* (1954) for writer-director Joseph L. Mankiewicz, playing a Hollywood director and one-time drunk making a comeback by turning gypsy dancer Ava

Gardner into a star under his tutelage. The film was a typically glossy Mankiewicz exercise and it won for Edmond O'Brien an Oscar for his performance as a venal press agent but, thanks to a pompous and at times depressingly pretentious script, the movie was more notable and enjoyable for the performances than for its content, and, at over two hours, it was painfully over-length. *Time* stated: 'The film has a few startlingly good lines and situations, and several embarrassingly bad ones, but even the neat lines, Bogart's expert delivery and some effectively acid scenes fail to make *Contessa* much more than an international-set soap opera'. The *Daily Telegraph* found it to be: 'A thinnish slice of the old baloney', liking, however, Bogart's 'harsh voice and ravaged face, which lifts the kindly director above facile sentimentality', and *The Times* said of him: 'Seldom has his air of weary disillusion been seen to better advantage.' The *Financial Times* crisply summed up *The Barefoot Contessa* as: '. . . this vastly blown-up example of the higher tosh.'

We're No Angels (1955) reunited Bogart with his old Warner Brothers director Michael Curtiz, now making this adaptation of the Broadway success for Paramount. He, Peter Ustinov and Aldo Ray were convicts who escape from Devil's Island and proceed to improve the lot of kindly Leo G. Carroll and his family instead of swindling them, and neatly dispose of villain Basil Rathbone in the process. The movie is undeniably stagey and the humour is mild, but Bogart, Ustinov and Ray play well together and, like its Christmas setting, the movie leaves one filled with good cheer. It was a pleasure to watch Bogart gently sending up his tough guy image from so many other films. Said *The Sunday Times*: 'The playing of the convicts is an unbroken delight. Unpromising though the material may sound, on the screen it is extremely funny.' And the *Daily Mail* noted that: 'Messrs Bogart, Ustinov and Ray are the most engaging trio of scoundrels who ever made crime seem a civilizing and comical way of life.' Other critics, however, appeared to object to the fact that Bogart was entertainingly sending himself and his gangster roles up with a wry and self-knowing skill.

The Desperate Hours (1955) saw Bogart – under William Wyler's direction – playing the role of an ageing gunman on the run from the law and holding Fredric March and his family captive in their home. Given that the premise was not too far removed from that of *The Petrified Forest* and like it, had been adapted by Joseph Hayes from his play

(and his novel), it should have been better than it turned out. Bogart himself, at a sneak preview of the movie, confided to director Wyler: 'Maybe I'm getting too old to play hoodlums.' In fact, his performance is superb and there are excellent supporting performances from Fredric March and Martha Scott, and much of the blame for the film's ultimate failure must lie with Wyler's innate good taste which was not really suited to the demands of the story.

'Bogart', said *Time*, 'gives a piteously horrible impression of the essential criminal', and the *Daily Herald* stated: 'Bogart . . . looks like an elderly, thin-lipped monkey, uses a voice of unvarying venom – and is right back at the top of the form that made him famous.' The *Evening Standard* liked his performance, saying: 'Bogart as the hoodlum leader gives one of the most unsympathetic performances of his career.'

If his next picture, *The Left Hand of God* (1955) has any claim to be admitted into the core of great Bogart movies, it can only be on account of the sheer silliness of the story and a performance by Lee J. Cobb as a Chinese war lord which is pure – if unintentional – comedy. Made for Twentieth Century-Fox under Edward Dmytryk's un-

involved direction, the movie cast Bogart as a Catholic priest in 1947 China, and looking extremely uncomfortable in a role that might have just about been convincing if it had been played by Barry Fitzgerald or Bing Crosby. Even the ultimate revelation that he was not a priest at all but a shot-down American airman did little to lighten the movie's plodding exposition. *Tribune* called it: '. . . a collector's piece for connoisseurs of the outrageous'. The *News Chronicle* found it: 'Unintentionally the year's best comedy from America', adding that: 'Mr Bogart looks and acts about as priestly as "Legs" Diamond', while *The Observer* thought: 'It says a good deal for Mr Bogart that he survives a killing part without discredit; but when he turns to Gene Tierney, the mission nurse who loves him, and observes, "I don't belong here, neither do you, we belong back in the States", it is very hard to disagree.' The studio publicists, as usual, thought differently, claiming in an advertisement: 'You count the TRULY DARING concepts in motion picture making in the

fingers of your right hand . . . *The Snake Pit, Pinky, Gentleman's Agreement, Ox Bow Incident, Grapes of Wrath*. NOW ADD *The Left Hand of God* – The story of a man who profaned the cloth he wore . . . and a woman who fought against a forbidden relationship! The most challenging story of faith ever told!' The only sensible reply to such hyperbole is 'Phooey' – particularly as the advertisement in question fails to point out that the films cited as being 'truly daring concepts in motion picture making' happen – coincidentally, no doubt – to be Twentieth Century-Fox films.

Bogart went to Columbia for his final film, *The Harder They Fall* (1956), directed by Mark Robson. Philip Yordan's screenplay was based on Budd Schulberg's novel exposing the fight game and Mike Lane, whose previous screen appearances had included the creature in *Frankenstein 70*, appeared as 'El Toro, The Wild Man of The Andes', a boxer with 'a powder puff punch and a glass jaw' who was pushed into a series of crooked fights by unscrupulous promoter Rod Steiger

to make him a contender for the heavyweight championship. Bogart played a world-weary unemployed sports writer hired by Steiger to help him in his scheme. Finally, Bogart was to blow the whistle on Steiger.

During the filming of *The Harder They Fall*, Bogart had several run-ins with Steiger, taking exception to his Method style of acting which involved physical jerks on-set before scenes and a great deal of muttering to himself. Bogart, the consummate professional, had no time for these antics, complaining to Jerry Wald (with whom he had worked in the old Warner Brothers days), that he couldn't work with Steiger, whose mumbling of his lines made Bogart miss his cues. 'Why the hell', he asked, 'don't they learn to speak properly? Words are important. This scratch-your-ass-and-mumble school of acting doesn't please me. You have to do something.'

What Bogart did was comfortably to steal the picture from Steiger, with a superb per-

formance that made his initial venality and his ultimate return to honesty both credible and moving. In a movie that featured several knock-down fights in the boxing ring, the real fight was the one for acting honours. This was won by Bogart, whose apparently effortless performance served to showcase his talent as an actor and make his last screen appearance a fitting epitaph to a memorable career. As for Steiger, he went down for the count time after time in their scenes together as he pulled out every Method trick in the book and succeeded only in going ludicrously over the top.

Bogart, who had always enjoyed needling people to see if they could take it, spent much of his time on the set needling Steiger who, reportedly, did not like the experience. But Bogart was glad to finish the film. He had felt tired and unwell most of the time – not that it showed in the finished film. *The Saturday Review* said that : 'Bogart does his usual high-quality job . . .' a sentiment

The Harder They Fall (Columbia) was Bogart's last picture and at least he had a credible part and gave a fine performance as a sports writer who double-crosses crooked boxing promoter Rod Steiger (left), who was attempting to groom a heavyweight contender by fixing fights.

echoed by the *Manchester Guardian* who stated: 'Humphrey Bogart has never done better in his harsh, leathery, and yet likable way . . .' Said the *Sunday Times*: 'Mr Steiger is surrounded by many lesser lights, each in his small way quite effective, actors who in repose still manage to threaten one's peace of mind. And all of them are overshadowed by Humphrey Bogart, whose cynical columnist remains the one anchor of humanity.'

Bogart's tiredness and constant coughing, which had plagued him during the making of *The Harder They Fall* were more serious than Bogart had realized and *The New York Times* reported on 28 February 1956: 'Humphrey Bogart said he would enter the Good Samaritan Hospital tomorrow to remove a slight obstruction on his esophagus', and went on to say that he hoped to leave hospital after about a week. There was also a report that his next picture would be *The Good Shepherd* and he and Betty were planning to make *Melville Goodwin, USA* together for Warner Brothers. The film would

later be filmed as *Top Secret Affair* with Kirk Douglas and Susan Hayward and it turned out to be a flop.

Bogart never worked again. He fought valiantly against the cancer that was destroying him, continuing to preside over the Holmby Hills Rat Pack whose members came to the house. Many of them found it painful to come, since it was clear that Bogart was dying, although Bogart himself faced death with an insolent bravery, appearing to treat it as simply one more difficult role to be taken on – and beaten.

But, at 2.10 am on 14 January 1957, Humphrey Bogart died.

Said *The New York Herald Tribune*: 'Mothers never held him up to children as their ideal, but youngsters relished his screen portrayals, and so, as a matter of fact, did their elders. In his fatal illness, Mr Bogart faced pain and tragedy with his customary boldness, even flippancy. He seemed to be defying fate to do its worst, and when it did, it found him calm and courageous. His death

Bogart, Best Actor for *The African Queen*, at the 1951 Oscar Awards with, from the left: Bette Davis (receiving Kim Hunter's Best Supporting Actress trophy), George Sanders (Best Supporting Actor of 1950), Karl Malden (Best Supporting Actor) and Greer Garson (receiving Best Actress Award for Vivien Leigh).

Far right: The star whose films are enjoyed as much now as when this typical portrait was taken in 1949, when he was at the height of his career.

Right: Bogart at the Savoy Hotel in 1953 receiving a British equivalent of the Oscar for his performance in *The African Queen*, with Olivia de Havilland, who was receiving an award on behalf of Susan Hayward for *With a Song in My Heart*.

robs the screen of a unique figure, and saddens thousands of his admirers . . .'

Fortunately, film gives its performers immortality of a kind, and today, long after his death, Bogart still lives in his movies and is probably as popular – if not more so – than he was at the height of his career. He was a great and unique star – and, for many, the greatest.

On 17 January 1957, Bogart's body was cremated at Forest Lawn Memorial Park and the funeral service at All Saints Episcopal Church, conducted by the Reverend Kermit Castellanos was attended by, among others, Gary Cooper, Spencer Tracy, Katharine Hepburn, Jack L. Warner, David O. Selznick, Billy Wilder, Harry Cohn, Jennifer Jones, Dick Powell and Danny Kaye and there was a crowd of some 3000 outside the church.

John Huston's farewell address summed up Bogart the man and the actor. 'With the years he had become increasingly aware of the dignity of his profession – Actor, not Star. Actor. Himself, he never took too seriously – his work, most seriously. He regarded the somewhat gaudy figure of Bogart the Star with an amused cynicism; Bogart the Actor he held in deep respect . . . His life, though not a long one measured in years, was a rich, deep life. He got what he asked for out of life – and more. He is quite irreplaceable. There will never be another like him'.

FILMOGRAPHY

Broadway's Like That. (Short). 1930. Vitaphone Corporation. Director: Murray Roth. With Ruth Etting, Joan Blondell.

A Devil with Women. 1930. Fox. Director: Irving Cummings. With Victor McLaglen, Mona Maris, Luana Alcaniz, Michael Vavitch.

Up the River. 1930. Fox. Director: John Ford. With Spencer Tracy, Claire Luce, Warren Hymer, William Collier Sr, Joan Marie Lawes, George MacFarlane, Gaylord Pendleton, Sharon Lynn.

Body and Soul. 1930. Fox. Director: Alfred Santell. With Charles Farrell, Elissa Landi, Myrna Loy, Donald Dillaway, Craufurd Kent, Pat Somerset, Ian MacLaren, Dennis D'Auburn.

Bad Sister. 1931. Universal. Director: Hobart Henley. With Conrad Nagel, Sidney Fox, Bette Davis, ZaSu Pitts, Slim Summerville, Charles Winninger, Emma Dunn, Bert Roach.

Women of All Nations. 1931. Fox. Director: Raoul Walsh. With Victor McLaglen, Edmund Lowe, Greta Nissen, El Brendel, Fifi Dorsay, Marjorie White, T. Roy Barnes, Bela Lugosi.

A Holy Terror. 1931. Fox. Director: Irving Cummings. With George O'Brien, Sally Eilers, Rita LaRoy, James Kirkwood, Robert Warwick, Richard Tucker, Stanley Fields.

Love Affair. 1932. Columbia. Director: Thornton Freeland. With Dorothy MacKaill, Jack Kennedy, Barbara Leonard.

Big City Blues. 1932. Warner Brothers. Director: Mervyn LeRoy. With Joan Blondell, Eric Linden, Inez Courtney, Evalyn Knapp, Guy Kibbee, Lyle Talbot, Gloria Shea, Walter Catlett, Jobyna Howland.

Three on a Match. 1932. First National-Warner Brothers. Director: Mervyn LeRoy. With Joan Blondell, Warren William, Ann Dvorak, Bette Davis, Lyle Talbot, Patricia Ellis, Glenda Farrell, Frankie Darro.

Midnight. 1934. All-Star/Universal. Director: Chester Erskine. With Sidney Fox, O. P. Heggie, Henry Hull, Margaret Wycherly, Lynne Overman, Katherine Wilson, Richard Whorf, Henry O'Neill.

The Petrified Forest. 1936. Warner Brothers. Director: Archie Mayo. With Leslie Howard, Bette Davis, Genevieve Tobin, Dick Foran, Joseph Sawyer, Porter Hall, Charley Grapewin, Paul Harvey, Eddie Acuff, Adrian Morris, Nina Campana, Slim Thompson.

Bullets or Ballots. 1936. First National-Warner Brothers. Director: William Keighley. With Edward G. Robinson, Joan Blondell, Barton MacLane, Frank McHugh, Joseph King, Richard Purcell.

Two Against the World (GB: *The Case of Mrs Pembrook.*) 1936. First National-Warner Brothers. Director: William McGann. With Beverly Roberts, Helen MacKellar, Henry O'Neill, Linda Perry, Virginia Brissac.

China Clipper. 1936. First National-Warner Brothers. Director: Ray Enright. With Pat O'Brien, Beverly Roberts, Ross Alexander, Marie Wilson, Henry B. Walthall, Joseph Crehan, Joseph King.

Isle of Fury. 1936. Warner Brothers. Director: Frank McDonald. With Margaret Lindsay, Donald Woods, Paul Graetz, Gordon Hart, E. E. Clive.

Black Legion. 1937. Warner Brothers. Director: Archie Mayo. With Dick Foran, Erin O'Brien-Moore, Ann Sheridan, Robert Barrat, Helen Flint, Joseph Sawyer, Addison Richards, Eddie Acuff, Clifford Soubier.

The Great O'Malley. 1937. Warner Brothers. Director: William Dieterle. With Pat O'Brien, Sybil Jason, Ann Sheridan, Frieda Inescort, Donald Crisp, Henry O'Neill, Craig Reynolds, Gordon Hart.

Marked Woman. 1937. First National-Warner Brothers. Director: Lloyd Bacon. With Bette Davis, Lola Lane, Isabel Jewell, Eduardo Cianelli, Rosalind Marquis, Mayo Methot, Jane Bryan, Allen Jenkins.

Kid Galahad. 1937. Warner Brothers. Director: Michael Curtiz. With Edward G. Robinson, Bette Davis, Wayne Morris, Jane Bryan, Harry Carey, William Haade, Soledad Cunningham, Veda Ann Borg, Ben Welden.

San Quentin. 1937. First National-Warner Brothers. Director: Lloyd Bacon. With Pat O'Brien, Ann Sheridan, Barton MacLane, Joseph Sawyer, Veda Ann Borg, James Robbins, Marc Lawrence, Joseph King.

Dead End. 1937. Sam Goldwyn/United Artists. Director: William Wyler. With Sylvia Sidney, Joel McCrea, Wendie Barrie, Claire Trevor, Allen Jenkins, Marjorie Main, Billy Halop, Huntz Hall, Bobby Jordan, Leo Gorcey, Gabriel Dell, Bernard Punsley, Ward Bond.

Stand-In. 1937. Walter Wanger/United Artists. Director: Tay Garnett. With Leslie Howard, Joan Blondell, Alan Mowbray, Marla Melton.

Swing Your Lady. 1938. Warner Brothers. Director: Ray Enright. With Frank McHugh, Louise Fazenda, Nat Pendleton, Penny Singleton, Allen Jenkins, Ronald Reagan, Leon Weaver, Frank Weaver, Sue Moore.

Crime School. 1938. First National-Warner Brothers. Director: Lewis Seiler. With Gale Page, Billy Halop, Bobby Jordan, Huntz Hall, Leo Gorcey, Bernard Punsley, Gabriel Dell, Charles Trowbridge.

Men Are Such Fools. 1938. Warner Brothers. Director: Busby Berkeley. With Priscilla Lane, Wayne Morris, Hugh Herbert, Penny Singleton.

The Amazing Dr Clitterhouse. 1938. First National-Warner Brothers. Director: Anatole Litvak. With Edward G. Robinson, Claire Trevor, Allen Jenkins, Donald Crisp, Gale Page, Maxie Rosenbloom, John Litel.

Racket Busters. 1938. Warner Brothers-Cosmopolitan. Director: Lloyd Bacon. With George Brent, Gloria Dickson, Allen Jenkins, Walter Abel.

Angels with Dirty Faces. 1938. First National-Warner Brothers. Director: Michael Curtiz. With James Cagney, Pat O'Brien, Ann Sheridan, George Bancroft, Billy Halop, Bobby Jordan, Leo Gorcey, Gabriel Dell, Huntz Hall, Bernard Punsley, Joseph Downing, Edward Pawley.

King of the Underworld. 1939. Warner Brothers. Director: Lewis Seiler. With Kay Francis, James Stephenson, John Eldredge, Jessie Busley.

The Oklahoma Kid. 1939. Warner Brothers. Director: Lloyd Bacon. With James Cagney, Rosemary Lane, Donald Crisp, Harvey Stephens, Hugh Sothern, Charles Middleton, Edward Pawley, Ward Bond.

Dark Victory. 1939. First National-Warner Brothers. Director: Edmund Goulding. With Bette Davis, George Brent, Geraldine Fitzgerald, Ronald Reagan, Henry Travers, Cora Witherspoon, Dorothy Peterson.

You Can't Get away with Murder. 1939. First National-Warner Brothers. Director: Lewis Seiler. With Billy Halop, Gale Page, John Litel, Henry Travers, Harvey Stephens, Harold Huber,

Joseph Sawyer.

The Roaring Twenties. 1939. Warner Brothers-First National. Director: Raoul Walsh. With James Cagney, Priscilla Lane, Gladys George, Jeffrey Lynn, Frank McHugh, Paul Kelly, Elisabeth Risdon.

The Return of Doctor X. 1939. First National-Warner Brothers. Director: Vincent Sherman. With Wayne Morris, Rosemary Lane, Dennis Morgan, John Litel, Lya Lys, Huntz Hall, Charles Wilson, Vera Lewis.

Invisible Stripes. 1939. Warner Brothers-First National. Director: Lloyd Bacon. With George Raft, Jane Bryan, William Holden, Flora Robson, Paul Kelly, Lee Patrick, Henry O'Neill, Marc Lawrence.

Virginia City. 1940. Warner Brothers-First National. Director: Michael Curtiz. With Errol Flynn, Miriam Hopkins, Randolph Scott, Frank McHugh, Alan Hale, Guinn 'Big Boy' Williams, Douglass Dumbrille.

It All Came True. 1940. Warner Brothers-First National. Director: Lewis Seiler. With Ann Sheridan, Jeffrey Lynn, ZaSu Pitts, Una O'Connor, Jessie Busley, John Litel, Grant Mitchell, Felix Bressart.

Brother Orchid. 1940. Warner Brothers-First National. Director: Lloyd Bacon. With Edward G. Robinson, Ann Sothern, Donald Crisp, Ralph Bellamy, Allen Jenkins, Cecil Kellaway, Morgan Conway.

They Drive by Night (GB: *The Road to Frisco*). 1940. Warner Brothers-First National. Director: Raoul Walsh. With George Raft, Ann Sheridan, Ida Lupino, Gale Page, Alan Hale, Roscoe Karns, John Litel, George Tobias, Paul Hurst.

High Sierra. 1941. Warner Brothers-First National. Director: Raoul Walsh. With Ida Lupino, Alan Curtis, Arthur Kennedy, Joan Leslie, Henry Hull, Henry Travers, Jerome Cowan, Minna Gombell.

The Wagons Roll at Night. 1941. Warner Brothers-First National. Director: Ray Enright. With Sylvia Sidney, Eddie Albert, Joan Leslie, Sig Rumann, Cliff Clark, Charley Foy, Frank Wilcox, John Ridgeley.

The Maltese Falcon. 1941. Warner Brothers-First National. Director: John Huston. With Mary Astor, Gladys George, Peter Lorre, Barton MacLane, Lee Patrick, Sydney Greenstreet, Ward Bond, Jerome Cowan, Elisha Cook Jr, James Burke, Murray Alper, Walter Huston.

All Through the Night. 1942. Warner Brothers-First National. Director: Vincent Sherman. With Conrad Veidt, Kaaren Verne, Jane Darwell, Frank McHugh, Peter Lorre, Judith Anderson, William Demarest.

The Big Shot. 1942. Warner Brothers-First National. Director: Lewis Seiler. With Irene Manning, Richard Travis, Susan Peters, Stanley Ridges, Minor Watson, Howard da Silva, Joseph Downing.

Across the Pacific. 1942. Warner Brothers-First National. Director: John Huston. With Mary Astor, Sydney Greenstreet, Charles Halton, Victor Sen Yung, Roland Got, Lee Tung Foo, Keye Luke, Frank Wilcox.

Casablanca. 1943. Warner Brothers-First National. Director: Michael Curtiz. With Ingrid Bergman, Paul Henreid, Claude Rains, Conrad Veidt, Sydney Greenstreet, Peter Lorre, S. Z. Sakall, Madeleine LeBeau, Dooley Wilson, Joy Page, John Qualen, Leonid Kinsky, Helmut Dantine, Curt Bois, Marcel Dalio, Corinna Mura, Dan Seymour.

Action in the North Atlantic. 1943. Warner Brothers-First National. Director: Lloyd Bacon. With Raymond Massey, Alan Hale, Julie Bishop, Ruth Gordon, Sam Levene, Dane Clark, Peter Whitney, Dick Hogan.

Thank Your Lucky Stars. 1943. Warner Brothers-First National. Director: David Butler. With Eddie Cantor, Bette Davis, Olivia de Havilland, Errol Flynn, John Garfield, Joan Leslie, Ida Lupino, Dennis Morgan, Ann Sheridan, Dinah Shore, Alexis Smith, Jack Carson, Alan Hale, George Tobias, Edward Everett Horton, S. Z. Sakall.

Sahara. 1943. Columbia. Director: Zoltan Korda. With Bruce Bennett, J. Carrol Naish, Lloyd Bridges, Rex Ingram, Richard Nugent, Dan Duryea, Carl Harbord, Patrick O'Moore.

Passage to Marseille. 1944. Warner Brothers-First National. Director: Michael Curtiz. With Claude Rains, Michele Morgan, Philip Dorn, Sydney Greenstreet, Peter Lorre, George Tobias, Helmut Dantine.

Report from the Front. 1944. Red Cross Drive Committee of the Motion Picture Industry. Trailer featuring Bogart and Mayo Methot in clips from their North African tour in December 1943.

To Have and Have Not. 1945. Warner Brothers-First National. Director: Howard Hawks. With Lauren Bacall, Walter Brennan, Dolores Moran, Hoagy Carmichael, Walter Molnar, Sheldon Leonard.

Conflict. 1945. Warner Brothers-First National. Director: Curtis Bernhardt. With Alexis Smith, Sydney Greenstreet, Rose Hobart, Charles Drake, Grant Mitchell, Patrick O'Moore, Ann Shoemaker.

Hollywood Victory Caravan. 1945. Paramount for the War Activities Committee and the Treasury Department. Director: William Russell. With numerous Hollywood stars and the US Maritime Service Training Station Choir. 20 minute movie about a war hero's sister's efforts to join a train carrying stars to Washington in which Bogart appealed for Victory Loan Bonds.

Two Guys from Milwaukee. 1946. Warner Brothers-First National. Director: David Butler. With Dennis Morgan, Jack Carson, Joan Leslie, Janis Paige, S. Z. Sakall. Bogart made a brief guest appearance.

The Big Sleep. 1946. Warner Brothers-First National. Director: Howard Hawks. With Lauren Bacall, John Ridgely, Martha Vickers, Dorothy Malone, Peggy Knudsen, Regis Toomey, Charles Waldron, Elisha Cook Jr, Charles D. Brown, Louis Jean Heydt, Sonia Darrin.

Dead Reckoning. 1947. Columbia. Director: John Cromwell. With Lizabeth Scott, Morris Carnovsky, Charles Cane, William Prince, Marvin Miller, Wallace Ford, James Bell.

The Two Mrs Carrolls. 1947. Warner Brothers-First National. Director: Peter Godfrey. With Barbara Stanwyck, Alexis Smith, Nigel Bruce, Isobel Elsom, Patrick O'Moore, Ann Carter, Anita Bolster.

Dark Passage. 1947. Warner Brothers-First National. Director: Delmer Daves. With Lauren Bacall, Bruce Bennett, Agnes Moorehead, Tom D'Andrea, Clifton Young, Douglas Kennedy, Rory Mallinson.

Always Together. 1948. Warner Brothers-First National. Director: Frederick de Cordova. With Robert Hutton, Joyce Reynolds, Cecil Kellaway, Ernest Truex. Bogart was seen in a film within the film.

The Treasure of the Sierra Madre. 1948. Warner Brothers-First National. Director: John Huston. With Walter Huston, Tim

Holt, Bruce Bennett, Barton MacLane, Alfonso Bedoya, John Huston, Jack Holt.

Key Largo. 1948. Warner Brothers-First National. Director: John Huston. With Edward G. Robinson, Lauren Bacall, Lionel Barrymore, Claire Trevor, Thomas Gomez, Harry Lewis, Marc Lawrence, Monte Blue.

Knock on any Door. 1949. Santana-Columbia. Director: Nicholas Ray. With John Derek, George Macready, Allene Roberts, Susan Perry, Mickey Knox, Barry Kelley, Cara Williams, Jimmy Conlin.

Tokyo Joe. 1949. Santana-Columbia. Director: Stuart Heisler. With Alexander Knox, Florence Marley, Sessue Hayakawa, Jerome Courtland, Gordon Jones, Teru Shimada, Hideo Mori.

Chain Lightning. 1950. Warner Brothers-First National. Director: Stuart Heisler. With Eleanor Parker, Raymond Massey, Richard Whorf, James Brown, Roy Roberts, Morris Ankrum, Fay Baker.

In a Lonely Place. 1950. Santana-Columbia. Director: Nicholas Ray. With Gloria Grahame, Frank Lovejoy, Carl Benton Reid, Art Smith, Jeff Donnell, Martha Stewart, Robert Warwick.

The Enforcer (GB: *Murder Inc.*). 1951. Warner Brothers. Director: Bretaigne Windust. With Zero Mostel, Ted De Corsia, Everett Sloane, Roy Roberts, Lawrence Tolan, King Donovan.

Sirocco. 1951. Santana-Columbia. Director: Curtis Bernhardt. With Marta Toren, Lee J. Cobb, Everett Sloane, Gerald Mohr, Zero Mostel, Nick Dennis, Onslow Stevens, Ludwig Donath.

The African Queen. 1951. Horizon-Romulus-United Artists. Director: John Huston. With Katharine Hepburn, Robert Morley, Peter Bull, Theodore Bikel, Walter Gotell, Gerald Onn.

Deadline – U.S.A. (GB: *Deadline*). 1952. Twentieth Century-Fox. Director: Richard Brooks. With Ethel Barrymore, Kim Hunter, Ed Begley, Warren Stevens, Paul Stewart, Martin Gabel.

Battle Circus. 1953. MGM. Director: Richard Brooks. With June Allyson, Keenan Wynn, Robert Keith, William Campbell, Perry Sheehan, Jonathan Cott, Adele Longmire, Ann Morrison.

Beat the Devil. 1954. Santana-Romulus-United Artists. Director: John Huston. With Jennifer Jones, Gina Lollobrigida, Robert Morley, Peter Lorre, Edward Underdown, Ivor Barnard.

The Caine Mutiny. 1954. Stanley Kramer-Columbia. Director: Edward Dymtryk. With Jose Ferrer, Van Johnson, Fred MacMurray, Robert Francis, May Wynn, Tom Tully, E. G. Marshall.

Sabrina (GB: *Sabrina Fair*). 1954. Paramount. Director: Billy Wilder. With Audrey Hepburn, William Holden, Walter Hampden, John Williams, Martha Hyer, Joan Vohs, Marcel Dalio.

The Barefoot Contessa. 1954. Figaro Incorporated. Director: Joseph L. Mankiewicz. With Ava Gardner, Edmond O'Brien, Marius Goring, Valentina Cortesa, Rosanno Brazzi, Elizabeth Sellars, Warren Stevens, Bessie Love.

We're No Angels. 1955. Paramount. Director: Michael Curtiz. With Aldo Ray, Peter Ustinov, Joan Bennett, Basil Rathbone, Leo G. Carroll, John Baer, Gloria Talbott, Lea Penman, John Smith.

The Left Hand of God. 1955. Twentieth Century-Fox. Director: Edward Dmytryk. With Gene Tierney, Lee J. Cobb, Agnes Moorehead, E. G. Marshall, Jean Porter, Carl Benton Reid, Victor Sen Yung.

The Desperate Hours. 1955. Paramount. Director: William Wyler. With Fredric March, Arthur Kennedy, Martha Scott, Dewey Martin, Gig Young, Mary Murphy, Richard Eyer, Robert Middleton.

The Harder They Fall. 1956. Columbia. Director: Mark Robson. With Rod Steiger, Jan Sterling, Mike Lane, Max Baer, Jersey Joe Walcott, Edward Andrews, Harold J. Stone, Nehemiah Persoff.

1983

To Todd Parker

Happy 19th birthday

with love
always
Grandma
&
Grampa
Parker